Self-Driven Learning

Teaching Strategies for Student Motivation

Larry Ferlazzo

EYE ON EDUCATION
6 DEPOT WAY WEST, SUITE 106
LARCHMONT, NY 10538
(914) 833–0551
(914) 833–0761 fax
www.eyeoneducation.com

For information about permission to reproduce selections from this book, write:
Eye On Education, Permissions Dept., Suite 106,
6 Depot Way West, Larchmont, NY 10538.

Library of Congress Cataloging-in-Publication Data

Ferlazzo, Larry.
  Self-driven learning : teaching strategies for student
motivation / by Larry Ferlazzo.
    pages cm
  ISBN 978-1-59667-239-0
 1. Motivation in education. 2. Effective teaching. 3. Classroom
management. I. Title.
  LB1065.F48 2013
  370.15′4--dc23

                                                    2012050287

10 9 8 7 6 5 4 3 2 1

Sponsoring Editor: Robert Sickles
Production Editors: Lauren Beebe and Lauren Davis
Copyeditor: Sarah Chassé
Designer and Compositor: Rick Soldin
Cover Designer: Dave Strauss, 3FoldDesign

Also Available from Eye On Education

Helping Students Motivate Themselves:
Practical Answers to Classroom Challenges
Larry Ferlazzo

Battling Boredom:
99 Strategies to Spark Student Engagement
Bryan Harris

75 Quick and Easy Solutions to Common Classroom Disruptions
Bryan Harris and Cassandra Goldberg

Making Good Teaching *Great*:
Everyday Strategies for Teaching with Impact
Annette Breaux and Todd Whitaker

What Great Teachers Do *Differently* (2nd Edition):
Seventeen Things That Matter Most
Todd Whitaker

Students Taking Charge:
Inside the Learner-Active, Technology-Infused Classroom
Nancy Sulla

The Passion-Driven Classroom:
A Framework for Teaching and Learning
Angela Maiers and Amy Sandvold

'Tween Crayons and Curfews:
Tips for Middle School Teachers
Heather Wolpert-Gawron

Reaching English Language Learners in Every Classroom:
Energizers for Teaching and Learning
Debbie Arechiga

101 "Answers" for New Teachers and Their Mentors (2nd Edition):
Effective Teaching Tips for Daily Classroom Use
Annette Breaux

Supplemental Downloads

All of the figures discussed and displayed in this book are also available on Eye On Education's website as Adobe Acrobat files. Permission has been granted to purchasers of this book to download these resources and print them.

You can access the downloads by visiting www.eyeoneducation.com. From the home page, click on the "Free" tab, then click on "Supplemental Downloads." Alternatively, you can search or browse our website for this book's product page, and click on "Log in to Access Supplemental Downloads."

Your book-buyer access code is **SDL-7-2390**.

Index of Supplemental Downloads

Contents

About the Author

Larry Ferlazzo teaches English and social studies to English language learners and mainstream students at Luther Burbank High School in Sacramento, California. He has written four previous books: *Helping Students Motivate Themselves: Practical Answers to Classroom Challenges*, *The ESL/ELL Teacher's Survival Guide* (with co-author Kaite Hull Sypnieski), *English Language Learners: Teaching Strategies That Work*, and *Building Parent Engagement in Schools* (with co-author Lorie Hammond).

Larry has won numerous awards, including the Leadership for a Changing World Award from the Ford Foundation, and was the grand prizewinner of the International Reading Association Award for Technology and Reading.

He writes a popular education blog (http://larryferlazzo.edublogs. org), a weekly teacher advice column for *Education Week Teacher*, and a monthly column for *The New York Times*. His articles on educational policy regularly appear in the *Washington Post* and the *Huffington Post*. His work has appeared in additional publications, including *ASCD Educational Leadership*, *Social Policy*, and *Language Magazine*.

Prior to becoming a public school teacher, Larry was a community organizer for nineteen years. He is married and has three children and two grandchildren.

Online Resources

Self-Driven Learning offers readers several online resources for further research, supplemental materials, and user involvement. For ease of access, these links have been posted on the book's product page on Eye On Education's website: **www.eyeoneducation.com**. From the home page, search by author or book title to locate the page for *Self-Driven Learning*. Then scroll to the bottom of the page and click on **Online Resources** for an index of easily clickable links.

Acknowledgments

I'd like to thank my family—Stacia, Rich, Shea, Ava, Nik, Karli, and especially my wife Jan—for their support. In addition, I need to express appreciation to my colleagues who have contributed to this book: Katie Hull Sypnieski, Carolyn Zierenberg, Dana Dusbiber, Lara Hoekstra, and Jim Peterson. I would also like to thank Kelly Young at Pebble Creek Labs and my many other colleagues at Luther Burbank High School, including Principal Ted Appel and Mai Xi Lee, for their assistance over the years. And, probably most important, I'd like to thank the many students who have made me a better teacher—and a better person. Finally, I must offer a big thank-you to Lauren Beebe, Lauren Davis, and Bob Sickles at Eye On Education for their patience and guidance in preparing this book.

Introduction

Why are you writing a second book on helping students motivate themselves?

It's been three years since *Helping Students Motivate Themselves* was published. Since then, I've spent more and more time thinking about the Michigan Fish Test, as it's been described by Columbia Business School professor Sheena Iyengar (2011).

She recounts a famous experiment in which researchers showed various groups a picture of three large fish in a sea scene. When people from the United States were asked to describe it, they focused on the large fish. When Japanese participants were asked to describe the same picture, they gave a much more holistic description of the picture. Iyengar suggests that it demonstrates the difference between the typical American individualistic approach and the more collectivist one found in Asian cultures. She writes: "The divergent accounts point to differing narratives of what controls what in the world, and how individual people fit into it" (Iyengar, 2011, para. 14).

It seems to me that this fish test is also an accurate metaphor for education today. In efforts to improve our schools, the emphasis often can be focused on those three "big fish"—changing teacher techniques to transmit information, moving toward prepackaged curriculum, and concentrating on "accountability" based on test scores from standardized tests.

But we can often lose sight of the bigger picture—of why students would want to learn what we're teaching in the classroom, why they would continue to want to study when they're not with us, how noncognitive character traits (self-control, perseverance, etc.) influence academic achievement and what we can do to help students develop them.

To borrow terms developed by political economist Albert O. Hirschman (Gladwell, 2012), if we do not reemphasize strategies to support the development of intrinsic motivation in our students, many are more likely to choose the option of "exit" (withdrawal from active engagement) over "voice" (active participation) in academic life.

Nobel laureate James Heckman is famous for his studies on the value of early childhood education. He demonstrates how important it is to help young children develop intrinsic motivation for character traits like self-control and perseverance and how that translates into academic and life success. Another one of his findings is less well-known, however—that there appears to be one other time in a child's life when he or she is particularly open to learning and applying these traits, and that time is adolescence (The Young Foundation, 2011).

The ideas in this book are designed for these adolescent learners (though many can be modified for other ages) and can be easily applied in the classroom and integrated into a regular curriculum.

Each chapter begins with a question related to a common classroom problem, which is followed by an imaginary (though real to most of us educators) complaint or concern voiced by a teacher.

Next is a section on immediate responses that teachers can take with little or no preparation to deal with a problem today, and those are accompanied with research supporting each suggested strategy. These portions of the chapter also include short mini-lessons—ones that are designed to take no longer than thirty minutes of class time. Three chapters—the ones on student motivation, classroom management, and higher-order thinking skills—elaborate on topics covered in *Helping Students Motivate Themselves* and also include sections on updating the strategies discussed in that volume.

A "setting the stage" section follows and provides short descriptions of lesson plans and the reasoning behind them. Each chapter then ends with the lesson plans themselves. Each lesson plan includes the Common Core Anchor State Standards for English Language Arts, Grades 6–12, that are covered by the lesson. Each chapter has suggestions on how to incorporate technology (in the Ed Tech sections). The URLs from lesson plans and Ed Tech sections are provided in an online document so you do not have to type them in manually (see page x for details).

The word *intrinsic* comes from the Latin *intrinsecus*, which is a combination of two Latin words meaning "within" and "alongside." All our students are intrinsically motivated—it just might not always be for doing what we want them to do. Our challenge is to work alongside our students and learn what their "self-interests"—goals, desires, dreams—might be and develop the trusting relationships needed to guide, extend, and expand them.

The strategies and lessons in this book are designed to be helpful tools that can be used along the way.

I Still Want to Know

How Do You Motivate Students?

Those ideas and lessons in the last book were good, and I continue to use them. However, colleagues in higher grades who are getting my students as they advance would like to reinforce developing intrinsic motivation with fresh lessons. I could use some additional ideas, too. What have you come up with since Helping Students Motivate Themselves *was published?*

Summary of the Case Against Emphasizing Extrinsic Rewards

This chapter, and this book, will share a number of ideas and lesson plans building on the foundational concept that "pushing the rope" of student motivation through external rewards is not in the best interest of our students, their families, or ourselves as educators.

Johann Wolfgang von Goethe's poem "The Sorcerer's Apprentice," made into the classic Disney film *Fantasia,* tells the story of an apprentice who is tired of doing the hard work of constantly carrying water into the house. When the sorcerer is away, the apprentice decides to take the easy way out and use magic he doesn't fully understand to make a broom fetch buckets of water. The spell works at first, but it ends up making things far worse when he can't make the broom stop and the house becomes flooded.

The use of carrots and sticks on a regular and systematic basis (though of course, there are *some* times when we all choose to use them) is one of those "magical solutions" that often ends up making things worse.

The application of these kinds of incentives has been proven time and time again to produce this "sorcerer's apprentice effect," as extensive research in *Helping Students Motivate Themselves* showed and new research in this book will reinforce. Professor Edward Deci is widely considered to be the most respected researcher in the field of motivation. He points out in *The New York Times* that his forty years of research shows that people will do something if they know how to do it and you pay them. But they'll stop doing it when you stop paying them, and in fact they'll then perform the behavior even less than they did before! The article continues:

> "There is no evidence that paying people helps them learn—and a lot of evidence that it doesn't," Deci said. Then why … resort to paying students? "Because it's easy," Deci said. "It's much harder to work with people to get them motivated from the inside." (Guttenplan, 2011, para. 18)

Author Daniel Pink (2009) describes how extrinsic rewards might work in the short term for mechanical tasks that don't require much higher-order thinking. But research shows that points, prizes, and presents don't tend to produce true motivation for any work that requires higher-order thinking skills and creativity.

Pink also points out that *everyone* needs "baseline rewards." These are the basics of adequate compensation. At school, students' baseline rewards might include fair grading, a caring teacher who works to provide engaging lessons, and a clean classroom. If baseline needs are not met, then a person's "focus will be on the unfairness of her situation and the anxiety of her circumstance. … You'll get neither the predictability of extrinsic motivation nor the weirdness of intrinsic motivation. You'll get very little motivation at all" (Pink, 2011a, p. 35).

In fact, recent research by Professor Armin Falk goes even further and finds that people who feel like they are not treated fairly do indeed feel increased motivation. However, they feel more motivated to do *worse* (Freeland, 2012)!

Does this book suggest that extrinsic motivators are always bad? No. On *some* occasions an extrinsic motivator can entice someone to try something new or can serve as way to deal with an immediate, one-student classroom problem without distracting the entire class.

The key, however, is to have an exit strategy in mind—one that will move your students in a relatively short time toward self-motivation. The suggestions in this book offer concrete ways to make that transition to a classroom culture of intrinsic motivation.

Recent Research on the Use of Rewards

Intrinsic motivation, sometimes also called autonomous motivation (Hout & Elliott, 2011, p. 30), is what the ideas and lessons in this book are designed to encourage. This kind of motivation drives students to put effort into learning because *they* see that it will help them achieve their personal goals.

Scores of studies—the National Academy of Sciences says at least 128, in fact—"showed clearly that tangible rewards do significantly and substantially undermine internal motivation" (Hout & Elliott, 2011, p. 26). Even reviews more sympathetic to the use of rewards in schools find that test gains are small and not sustained over time (Usher & Kober, 2012, p. 9). One well-publicized study that claimed to show giving cash or trophies would result in increased test gains (though they were not sustainable) found that it worked best if students were given the reward prior to taking the test and told it would be taken away if test scores did not improve (Levitt, List, Neckermann, & Sadoff, 2011). Here's an excerpt from a television interview with one of the authors, Dr. Sally Sadoff:

> **Q:** The ones that did badly—did you rip it away from them and then did they scream and cry?
>
> **A:** Yeah, it's hard when you rip a trophy out of the hands of an eight-year-old.
>
> ("Is Bribing Students," 2012)

It's questionable whether an incentive system like that would contribute toward building a positive classroom culture.

One particularly intriguing study was published in 2011. It found that just mentioning the idea of rewards as a possible motivating tool (in that case, money) actually resulted in the participants in the experiment wanting to do the exact opposite of what they were asked to do (Pink, 2012). Another recent study reached the same conclusion—half of Swiss citizens who originally supported a nuclear waste facility in the community changed their minds when they were told they would receive money for their support (Rothman, 2012)—they said they could not be bribed.

Ed Tech
Motivation Research

For a complete review of research on motivation, rewards, and incentives, including several insightful and funny video clips from popular television programs that highlight key concepts, go to "The Best Posts & Articles On 'Motivating' Students" (www.larryferlazzo.edublogs.org/2010/05/17/my-best-posts-on-motivating-students).

Using points, grades, and percentages as motivational levers might not always get the desired effect from all our students.

Updates on "Old" Strategies

Helping Students Motivate Themselves included many suggested immediate actions and several lessons plans in the student motivation chapter and elsewhere. All of them won't be repeated here, but some will be reviewed and supplemented with updated information.

Engaging Lessons

Engaging lessons are an important part of the baseline rewards mentioned earlier in this chapter. Boring lessons don't encourage the development of intrinsic motivation!

Recent research has reinforced the effectiveness of cooperative and discovery learning, and demonstrated the weaknesses of lectures and direct instruction (of course, that's not to suggest that direct instruction should *never* be used, but it should certainly have a subordinate role).

One 2011 meta-analysis of hundreds of studies (Alfieri, Brooks, Aldrich, & Tenenbaum, 2011) highlighted by education researcher Robert Marzano (2011) found that "enhanced discovery learning" was clearly superior to direct instruction. The study identified three kinds of "enhanced discovery learning methods"—"generation, elicited explanations, and guided discovery conditions"—and defined them in this way:

> Generation conditions required learners to generate rules, strategies, images, or answers to experimenters' questions. Elicited explanation conditions required that learners explain some aspect of the target task or target material, either to themselves or to the experimenters. The guided discovery conditions involved either some form of instructional guidance (i.e., scaffolding) or regular feedback to assist the learner at each stage of the learning tasks. (p. 5)*

This definition certainly describes the inductive learning process, which is explained in lessons plans in the chapters on classroom management, on higher-order thinking skills, and on reading and writing, and was also extensively

---

*Does discovery-based instruction enhance learning? *Journal of Educational Psychology, 103*(1), 1–18.) Copyright © 2011 by the American Psychological Association. Reproduced [or Adapted] with permission. The use of APA information does not imply endorsement by APA.)

described in *Helping Students Motivate Themselves*.

It should be pointed out that this same analysis found that direct instruction was a more effective method than *unassisted* discovery learning, which is students learning on their own with very little teacher assistance. An example might be teaching the scientific method by first giving students scissors and two cups, one half filled with water, and asking them to figure out how they would tell time using the items. Many teachers might start off a lesson this way—plenty of research (Wolfe, 2001, p. 82) has shown that the use of novelty like this *is* effective—though few would probably make the whole lesson unassisted. The study defined unassisted discovery learning as an entire lesson following that process.

Ed Tech
Research and Examples of Engaging Lessons

Links to extensive research on cooperative learning and discovery learning can be found at "The Best Sites for Cooperative Learning" (www.larryferlazzo.edublogs.org/2010/04/02/the-best-sites-for-cooperative-learning-ideas) and at "The Best Posts Questioning If Direct Instruction is 'Clearly Superior'" (www.larryferlazzo.edublogs.org/2012/04/30/the-best-posts-questioning-if-direct-instruction-is-clearly-superior). Both lists include videos of lessons in action.

Robert Slavin has added to the extensive research available documenting the effectiveness of cooperative learning in "Co-operative Learning: What Makes Group-Work Work?" (2010), and Harvard professor Eric Mazur's work on moving away from lecture and using more cooperative peer instruction has received widespread attention recently (Hanford, 2011).

Choice and Ownership

People are more motivated when they have more control over their environment (Rigoglioso, 2008). In an experiment documented by Nobel Prize winner Daniel Kahneman, which has since been repeated many times, half the participants in a lottery were given random numbers. The other half were given pieces of paper and could write whatever numbers they wished. Researchers then offered to purchase the tickets. They found that they had to pay those who wrote their own numbers five times what they had to pay those who were given numbers. In other words, experiments have found that having the ability to choose for ourselves makes us five times more committed to—and invested in—the outcome than if someone else chooses for us (Keller, 2012b).

A different, and very recent, study reemphasizes the importance of choice in the classroom for most students. Researchers found that power and choice were interchangeable, since both deal with the issue of control; having more of one could compensate for having less of the other (American Psychological Association, 2011).

There are many things we can do in the classroom to help our students feel like they have power—for example, involving them in decisions on issues like seating or even room arrangement. But those efforts can appear tiny in situations where students are immigrants whose parents moved them to a new country or come from low-income families and feel they have little power to confront multiple economic and social challenges.

However, in addition to our possibly feeble efforts to help engage students in feeling powerful, we can certainly emphasize offering choices—the kinds of homework they have to do, the types of presentations they can organize, the essay topics they can respond to, and so on.

The payoff can be students who are happier and more open to learning and to accepting challenges—not to mention an easier classroom-management situation for the teacher.

Another recent study seconded this endorsement of choice. Students in Texas were given the choice of two homework assignments covering the same material. The researcher wrote: "When students were given choices, they reported feeling more interested in their homework, felt more confident about their homework and they scored higher on their unit tests" (Sparks, 2010, para. 5).

The Brain Is Like a Muscle

Helping students understand that the brain is like a muscle that gets stronger with use (Dweck, 2008) can be an important step in developing intrinsic motivation. It highlights the fact that intelligence is not fixed and helps students understand that their brain cells physically grow as they learn new things. A well-publicized study in 2011 demonstrated that this growth continues throughout the teenage years (Sparks, 2011). Stanford professor Carol Dweck describes these perspectives as the difference between a "fixed mind-set" and a "growth mind-set."

> These beliefs can influence what happens when you encounter information that feels hard to learn. Someone who believes intelligence is a talent will feel that they have reached their limit when they encounter something hard, and that should make them feel like they can't learn it. Someone who believes that intelligence is a skill will feel that difficult information is a challenge they can overcome. (Markman, 2011, para. 7)

In fact, recent studies have shown having a growth mind-set actually generates greater electric neural signals in our brains. The brain signals in those who believe they can improve with experience focus more:

> attention to mistakes. And the larger that neural signal, the better subsequent performance. That mediation suggests that individuals with an incremental theory of intelligence may actually have better self-monitoring and control systems on a very basic neural level: their brains are better at monitoring their own, self-generated errors and at adjusting their behavior accordingly. (Konnikova, 2012a, para. 6)

Or, as journalist Jonah Lehrer (2011) summarized the study: "Because the subjects were thinking about what they got wrong, they learned how to get it right" (para. 8).

Helping students see that their brains grow by learning can have a powerful impact. Now, in addition, students can learn that they are actually capable of altering the electric neural signals in their brains *based on what they believe.*

The "Mistakes and the Brain" mini-lesson highlights this new research about how making mistakes affects the brain:

Mini-Lesson: Mistakes and the Brain

The read-aloud in Figure 1.1, page 8, summarizes a study exploring how our beliefs about learning affect the electrical signals in our brains. It can be used as a stand-alone lesson or as a follow-up to lessons in *Helping Students Motivate Themselves.*

1. The teacher can ask everyone who has ever made a mistake to raise a hand (and the teacher can raise his or her hand, as well). The teacher explains that, of course, we all make mistakes.

2. The teacher quickly explains the difference between a fixed mind-set and a growth mind-set. The first is the belief that you're born with whatever intelligence you have (the teacher could say one student described it as "you're born as smart or as dumb as you're ever going to get"), and the second is the belief that you get smarter by hard work. If you have a fixed mind-set, when you make a mistake you just figure that you're not smart enough to do something right. If you have a growth mind-set, you think making a mistake is just another opportunity to learn to get better at doing something.

3. The teacher places the read-aloud on the overhead and asks students to read along silently as he or she reads it to the class.

Figure 1.1   Read-Aloud: What Does Learning from Mistakes Do to the Brain?

A Michigan State University professor measured the electrical activity in the brains of groups of two different kinds of people: some who believed that intelligence was fixed (you're born with a certain amount of intelligence and that's it) and others who believed that intelligence could be improved with hard work. Both groups were put into situations where they made mistakes.

The group of people who believed that intelligence could be improved with hard work—the people with a "growth mind-set"—had greater electrical brain activity when evaluating those mistakes. In other words, their neural signals showed that their brains were putting more energy into figuring out what the mistake was and how they could fix it. They were noticing the errors faster and correcting them more quickly.

Journalist Jonah Lehrer described it like this: "Because the subjects were thinking about what they got wrong, they learned how to get it right."

Sources: Konnikova (2012a, February 18) & Lehrer (2011, October 4)

4. The teacher asks students to take a minute and think about this question: "What do you think he meant by 'Because the subjects were thinking about what they got wrong, they learned how to get it right'?"

5. The teacher then has students share their responses quickly with a partner and asks a few students to share with the class.

6. Next, the teacher explains that he or she is going to ask students to respond to this question, which he or she writes on the overhead: "Think of a time in your life, or in the life of someone you've read about, where you or that person learned from a mistake. What happened?"

7. The teacher gives students three minutes to write answers to the question, has students share them with a partner, and then has a few share with the class.

8. The teacher ends by suggesting that students look at making mistakes as an opportunity to learn, and writes this quote from journalist and surgeon Atul Gawande (2012) on the board and reads it aloud: "A failure often does not have to be a failure at all. However, you have to be ready for it—will you admit when things go wrong? Will you take steps to set them right?—because the difference between triumph and defeat, you'll find, isn't about willingness to take risks. It's about mastery of rescue" (para. 26).

Ed Tech
Brain Videos

Several short and engaging videos that are accessible to students and show how brain cells grow when people learn new things can be found at "The Best Resources For Showing Students That They Make Their Brain Stronger By Learning" (www.larryferlazzo.edublogs. org/2011/11/26/the-best-resources-for-showing-students-that-they-make-their-brain-stronger-by-learning/). Updated research on brain-based learning can also be found there.

Praise for Effort

Teachers should praise the effort and not the intelligence of their students (Bronson, 2007) in order to help students develop a growth mind-set. Praising for intelligence makes people less willing to risk what Dweck calls "their newly minted genius status" (as cited in Rock, 2011, para. 10), while praising effort encourages the idea that we primarily learn through our hard work: "Johnny, that was impressive that you did two drafts of that essay. What made you want to put that extra effort into it?"

There are multiple opportunities each day to praise students for effort. I make a point of doing so during my favorite time of the school week. Once a week during lunchtime, I walk around campus looking for students I have taught or am currently teaching. Usually they are with their friends. I walk up to the group, point out that student, and say something like, "Did you know that there is no harder worker in my class than _____?" or "Did you know that there are few other students who help their classmates more than _____?" or some other comment singling out that particular student for something that they do especially well.

Those students, though they may feign embarrassment, love it. In fact, it's not unusual for one of their friends whom I don't know to say, "What about me?" I quickly respond, "If you were in my class, I'm sure I could say the same thing about you."

I have, and continue to have, many students who face lots of challenges, and it's safe to say that many don't get the kind of positive feedback they deserve. A little public acknowledgment can go a long way. However, it's not effective to praise effort when a student did not successfully accomplish the task or learn the concept. Students can generally see through that type of fake feedback. In those cases, research suggests that it is best to focus on "purely informational feedback" to help the student figure out the problem (Halvorson, 2011). Dr. Robert Brooks suggests that this kind of informational feedback be prefaced with a "we" statement such as "This strategy you're using doesn't seem to be working. Let's figure out why and how we can change the strategy so that you are successful" (Brooks, as cited in Washburn, 2009, para. 11).

Progress Principle

Dweck (2010) also suggests that creating opportunities for students to clearly see the growth in their own knowledge advances a growth mindset. Ways to make this happen include having students write what they know about a subject at the beginning of a unit, collecting that writing, and then giving it back at the unit's end so they can see how much they learned.

This important concept was referred to as "the progress principle" in a 2011 book of the same name by Teresa Amabile and Steven Kramer. In an ambitious study examining the diaries of hundreds of employees, the authors concluded "that, of all the events that have the power to excite people and engage them in their work, the single most important is making progress—even if that progress is a small win. That's the progress principle" (Pink, 2011b, para. 7).

Goal Setting

Several of the lesson plans in this book have specific goal-setting activities connected to them. Here is a review of some of the reasoning and research behind those lesson elements:

Students setting their own goals can enhance intrinsic motivation, especially if they distinguish between learning goals ("I want to read more challenging books" or "I want to be more of a leader in small groups") and performance goals ("I want to get an A in this class") (Latham & Locke, 2006, p. 334). A review of one hundred studies found that students focusing on learning goals were the ones who achieved better academic grades (Viadero, 2010).

Other key qualities in successful goal setting (and goal reaching) include reviewing goals regularly; framing goals as questions ("Will We Succeed," 2010) and then responding ("Will I be a leader in small groups?" "Yes!"); having the support of a partner (Kristof, 2009) and meeting regularly for mutual support (Economic & Social Research Council, 2012; Shteynberg & Galinsky, in press); making goals public (DiSalvo, 2010); and designing actions to reach those goals.

Two newer studies have pointed out a few additional things to keep in mind. One supports what common sense tells most of us—that the fewer goals we make, the higher the likelihood of achieving them (Markman, 2012b). This finding is an important one for us to emphasize to our students.

The second study is more intriguing. It found that self-motivation was increased by visualizing progress toward achieving goals—not visually in the sense of imagining it in your mind (see "Chapter 2: What Can You Do to Help Students Feel More Positive About School And Learning?" for information on that idea), but by actually drawing and updating a personal graph or chart and updating it ("Easy to Visualize," 2011). Having students create these kinds of charts for themselves (not necessarily for public sharing) and regularly update them would certainly be easy to do.

The goal-setting process described here, along with this kind of continual student self-evaluation of progress toward achieving goals, has been found to be a key ingredient in students developing a greater sense of self-efficacy. This belief in their own competence is another driver of intrinsic motivation (Schunk & Meece, 2005, p. 79).

Relevance

As William Glasser (1988) and others have found, many students "will not work to learn" (p. 21) unless they can see the lessons as helpful to their goals. Recent research has reinforced that finding.

A study had students write one paragraph after a lesson sharing how they thought what they learned would be useful in their lives. Writing one to eight of these during a semester led to positive student learning gains (Hulleman & Harackiewicz, 2009).

"New" Strategies for Immediate Responses

Here are several strategies—not discussed in *Helping Students Motivate Themselves*—to enhance student intrinsic motivation that teachers can keep in mind during day-to-day work in the classroom.

Flow

Flow is the term developed by Hungarian psychologist Mihaly Csikszentmihalyi to describe the feeling of being totally immersed in the task at hand, losing track of time, and experiencing great feelings of satisfaction with what you are doing (Mihaly Csikszentmihalyi on flow, 2004).

Professor David Shernoff has done extensive research applying the idea of flow to the classroom. He has found that—apart from when students might be working at a relatively mindless paying job, like flipping hamburgers—young people are least likely to experience this sense of flow in the classroom (Bronson, 2009).

He has identified several strategies that teachers could implement to help change that perspective, including:

♦ developing good teacher-student relationships

♦ helping students clearly see the relevance of lessons to their lives and to student-created goals

♦ providing challenging assignments that students are adequately prepared to accomplish

♦ giving regular and supportive feedback to students during the assignment

♦ creating an interactive environment—in other words, minimal lecture time

♦ demonstrating a good sense of humor

♦ supporting students' autonomy by allowing students to choose their assignments or how to do them ("Education Professor Writes," 2010)

Most of these elements have already been discussed in this chapter. By putting them all together—admittedly, not an easy thing to do in the midst of a crazy school day—perhaps we can increase the odds of our students experiencing flow a little more often in the classroom.

Using Descriptive Norms

Descriptive norms are what people think are the common forms of behavior in a particular situation. A study on this concept found that in a hotel, people were far more likely to keep their towels for an extra day if a sign said, "'75 percent of the guests who stayed in this room (room 313)' had reused their towels" than if it contained a general appeal to save the environment (Mindlin, 2008, para. 2).

Using this idea occasionally in the classroom (in a truthful and not deceiving way) may help students *want* to try new things. For example, a teacher could introduce a book to a student by explaining that it was one of the more popular ones in the class during the previous year. The "Visualization Lesson Plan" in Chapter 2 could also by introduced by saying that students who have taken the lesson seriously in previous years achieved more of their goals than those who did not.

The Zeigarnik Effect

Bluma Zeigarnik, a Russian psychologist, identified what has come to be called the Zeigarnik effect ("The Zeigarnik Effect," 2011): Once we start doing something, we tend to want to finish it. Psychologists have also called this a need for closure; our minds naturally tend to not want to leave things unfinished (Konnikova, 2012c).

How can we use this in the classroom? One important way is to introduce students to the Zeigarnik effect in a very short mini-lesson so it becomes a tool in their toolbox of strategies to use when they are having a difficult time getting started on a project. This mini-lesson could be as simple as a teacher explaining what the Zeigarnik effect is, telling a story about when he or she has applied it in his or her life, asking students to think about times when it worked for them, and then doing a quick classroom sharing.

And, if some students forget the Zeigarnik effect when they are facing challenging assignments, teachers can remind students of it and help them think of different ways to get started: answering the first question, starting off by completing the easiest task, or using a graphic organizer to map out a concept prior to writing about it.

Writing a Blog

I write a blog. Among other things, I write about my students—in a positive way (and I change the names). I believe it sends an important message to students that I think about them when they aren't in my classroom. In addition, students often say they like the fact that what they do in class could influence what other teachers reading the blog do, and many comment that they want to be good examples for those who will read about them.

And research suggests that we should expect these reactions.

The Hawthorne effect refers to a series of studies that showed how workers would increase their productivity with multiple variables, and is generally thought to show that participants in a research project might be influenced just by knowing somebody is watching. The original studies showed that this knowledge is more important than if, for example, the lights on the factory floor are darker or brighter. Joanne Yatvin, a past president of the National Council of Teachers of English, described the Hawthorne effect in a slightly different way:

> The Hawthorne anomaly illustrates the fact that human subjects
> who know they are part of a scientific experiment may sabotage the

study in their eagerness to make it succeed. What it really shows is that, when people believe they are important in a project, anything works, and, conversely, when they don't believe they are important, nothing works. (Strauss, 2011, para. 8)

Of course, there are other ways besides a blog to have students believe their actions in class have wider implications. Teachers could devise a simple teacher research action project that they could then share with their colleagues (Heflebower, 2009; Mettetal, 2002–2003)—for example, having students do a reflection journal or spending five minutes more a day in class reading for pleasure; the possibilities are limitless. Perfectly reliable and valid results are less important than students knowing that they are part of something special!

Clear and Easy-to-Read Instructions

Having instructions written in clear print that is easy for students to read can make them feel more motivated to want to do an assignment. That is the conclusion drawn from two experiments in which instructions were given for cooking and for exercising in easy-to-read typeface and in harder-to-read font. In both cases, participants who read the clearer words were more motivated to do the work (Herbert, 2009).

Neat teacher handwriting or typed instructions in a simple font can pay off!

Giving Advice

Most teachers are not shy about giving advice to students—whether they ask for it or not! But what is the best way to give advice?

A recent study suggests that people are more likely to listen to advice that provides information they don't already know, rather than a simple recommendation for or against something (Dalai & Bonaccio, 2010). Professor Art Markman suggests that there are three reasons why new information is the preferred advice form: it promotes autonomy in the advice seekers; it provides them with knowledge they might be able to use during other times, too; and it helps them feel more confident in the decisions they ultimately make by giving them new reasons they can use for justification (Markman, 2012c).

Of course, if we really want to promote student autonomy, we probably want to combine giving information with asking questions that would help the advice seeker clarify his or her own thinking (Bluestein, n.d.).

Whatever we do, though, the question we should ask ourselves—in the case of giving advice and in many other areas—is: Do we want to be right, or do we want to be effective? We may feel we know what the correct course of action is for our students, and every part of us wants to tell them what we know, but restraint and patience may very well be what the student needs for short- and long-term confidence and competence.

Plants

Research, and probably personal experience, shows that we can spend only so much time focusing on a task before attention begins to fade and performance declines, and that short breaks help us refocus again ("Brief Diversions," 2011). Attention restoration theory suggests that experiencing nature briefly can provide a particularly helpful break, and research shows that just looking at a houseplant can offer a helpful restorative experience (Riddle, 2011).

As teachers you might want to share this information with your students—whether or not you have plants in your classroom. Encouraging students to take short breaks of even a minute when they feel their performance is slipping because of sustained concentration might be worth trying in class.

One-Sentence Project

Daniel Pink suggests that one way people can clarify their lives' goals and to center on the intrinsic motivation required to achieve them is to develop "one sentences" for themselves (Pink, 2011a, p. 154). His idea was inspired by a story about Congresswoman Clare Boothe Luce telling President John F. Kennedy that "a great man is one sentence." She is said to have given the example that President Abraham Lincoln's sentence was: "He preserved the union and freed the slaves." She was concerned that Kennedy was trying to do too many things and was not clear on his priorities.

Pink's idea for people to develop their own "one sentences" ("He raised five happy children." "She taught hundreds of children to read." "She discovered the cure for cancer.") has been applied in workplaces and schools across many countries.

It's similar to the old exercise suggesting that people think about how they want others to describe them after they're gone and then live backward. It's goal setting, but with an intriguing twist, which is why it is here in the new strategies section.

Of course, once students create their sentences, they can regularly use them as reflective tools, asking: What did I do today to bring me closer to achieving that one sentence? What can I do tomorrow to do the same?

Authentic Audience

Writing a document or creating another kind of product that will be seen by only one person—the teacher—sometimes does not generate the highest level of motivation from students to produce their best work.

Recent research shows that students became more concerned about the accuracy and quality of their work if they knew it would be posted online ("Wikipedia Improves," 2011). Even if that is not an option, students can present their work in small groups (a series of presentations to an entire class has the potential of being fairly deadly); share it with "sister classes" in the same school or in another location; or write letters to the editor.

Setting the Stage

This section contains two short and engaging lesson plans designed to help students develop their intrinsic motivation. Each lesson incorporates higher-order thinking, Common Core State Standards, and literacy instruction with complex texts and cooperative learning. In addition, the lessons also suggest ways to periodically reflect on them throughout the school year.

Teaching Others

Many of us have heard this saying: "We learn 10 percent of what we read, 20 percent of what we hear, 30 percent of what we see, 50 percent of what we see and hear, 70 percent of what we say or write, and 90 percent of what we teach." The usual source cited is Edgar Dale's Cone of Experience. Unfortunately, it bears little resemblance to the Cone that Dale developed in 1946, which didn't include any percentages or any research to back it up (Thalheimer, 2006).

The maxim may make intuitive sense to many of us, though, and fortunately there has been research that at least provides evidence demonstrating the importance of the last category—learning through teaching. Several studies have shown that this kind of "self-explanation" is a particularly effective learning strategy (Konnikova, 2012b).

There are many ways to incorporate this kind of learning-through-teaching strategy in classroom lessons: "jigsaw" presentations, in which small groups are given different sections of textbook chapter or different portions of a famous figure's life and then teach what they have learned; a quick pair-share exercise where students explain to each other a newly learned concept; or a "sister class" situation where native English speakers teach a grammar lesson to English language learners, and then ELLs, in turn, teach something about their native culture.

The "Teaching Others Lesson Plan" (page 19) however, combines this concept with elements of another one to maximize its self-motivational potential. It uses the idea of Innovation Days or Genius Hours (formerly known as "Fed Ex Days" because an Australian company periodically gave their employees twenty-four hours to work on projects of their own choosing as long as they "delivered" what they had worked on "overnight"—in twenty-four hours). Teachers throughout the world have adapted this concept to allow students to pursue topics of high interest to *them* (and related to the classroom subject). Educators have also applied the concept to professional development.

Creating an opportunity for students to learn about topics of their own choosing, develop lesson plans that force them to think through how best to communicate what they have learned and what they want others to learn from them, and then actually teach includes most of the elements listed earlier that help develop student self-efficacy.

The "Student-Created Unit Lesson Plan" in *Helping Students Motivate Themselves* (p. 106) has many similarities to this new "Teaching Others

Lesson Plan." That previous lesson has a duration of ten to fifteen class periods and has students choose their own topics, create completed unit plans using a limited list of instructional strategies, and teach small parts of those units. The unit plans are designed as end-of-year projects.

The intent behind this "Teaching Others Lesson Plan," on the other hand, is for students to become familiar with a broader range of instructional strategies and the research behind them. Then, they can choose topics and apply several of those teaching strategies. Moreover, this lesson plan can be completed within five class periods, and can be repeated in even less time during the year.

This process provides opportunities for students to read challenging text related to topics of their choice and practice public speaking skills. They will have to utilize the higher levels of Bloom's Taxonomy throughout the lesson. More importantly—and this is a primary purpose of the lesson—students will gain a much greater grasp of the *reasons* teachers do what they do and, as a result, could become more invested in fully participating in class lessons throughout the year. They will also get a taste of the many challenges teachers face, including the 0.7 decisions teachers have to make per minute (Cuban, 2011) and, ideally, become more motivated to want to contribute toward creating a supportive learning environment in the classroom. In addition, if desired, teachers can regularly ask students to reflect on classroom lessons and request feedback from them about how they could be improved—using what they learned in this lesson about effective instructional strategies as their context.

Power is not a finite thing. Letting students in on some of our "secret sauce" does not mean we will have less power as teachers. In fact, the entire pie gets bigger by creating additional learning opportunities for teachers and students alike.

Ed Tech
Innovation Days and Genius Hours

The emphasis in the "Teaching Others Lesson Plan" is on the teaching part of what students have learned or created, while, traditionally, Innovation Days and Genius Hours place the emphasis on the learning/creating part and less on structuring the sharing aspect of the event. The two things they have in common are basing the topics on student interest and having a short turnaround time. Of course, teachers always have the option of trying out this idea in multiple ways. Examples of how a variety of educators have implemented different versions can be found at "The Best Resources For Applying 'FedEx Days' To Schools" (www.larryferlazzo.edublogs.org/2012/05/28/the-best-resources-for-applying-fed-ex-days-to-schools).

Teaching Others Lesson Plan

Instructional Objectives for Students:

- Read a challenging text describing instructional strategies and apply reading strategies to aid comprehension.

- Research topics of their choice and develop and then teach lessons applying those instructional strategies.

- Write short opinion paragraphs and back up their positions with evidence.

Duration: Five sixty-minute class periods the first time the lesson is done. If it's done again during the year, it should not be necessary to repeat the first two days, so the entire lesson can be done in two and half or three days.

Materials:

- Document camera or overhead projector with screen

- Internet connection to projector (optional)

- Copies for each student of "Question 8: What Are the Best Things You Can Do to Maximize the Chances of a Lesson Being Successful?" from *Helping Students Motivate Themselves.* A PDF of the chapter can be found in the downloadable resources for this book (see page v for details).

- Several sheets of easel paper and colored markers

- Access to a computer lab during the third day for student research

- Student copies of a teacher-created graphic organizer for the jigsaw, if desired

- Student copies of Figure 1.2, Figure 1.3, Figure 1.4, and Figure 1.5 (pages 25–28)

Common Core English Language Arts Standards

Reading: Determine central ideas or themes of a text and analyze their development; summarize the key supporting details and ideas.

Writing: Produce clear and coherent writing in which the development, organization, and style are appropriate to task, purpose, and audience.

Speaking and Listening:

- Prepare for and participate effectively in a range of conversations and collaborations with diverse partners, building on others' ideas and expressing their own clearly and persuasively.

- Adapt speech to a variety of contexts and communicative tasks, demonstrating command of formal English when indicated or appropriate.

Language:

- Demonstrate command of the conventions of standard English grammar and usage when writing or speaking.

- Demonstrate command of the conventions of standard English capitalization, punctuation, and spelling when writing.

Procedure

First Day:

1. Students enter the room with the image on the screen of the classroom blackboard of Nobel Prize–winning physicist Richard Feynman on the day he died. It says "What I cannot create, I do not understand" (http://blogs.scientificamerican.com/literally-psyched/2012/04/07/hunters-of-myths-why-our-brains-love-origins/).

2. The teacher briefly explains who Feynman was and puts a sheet under the document camera with that sentence typed out clearly, reads it out loud, and then asks students to take two minutes to think about and write what they think he meant.

3. The teacher walks around the classroom and identifies a few students he or she might call on later to share. He or she then asks students to verbally share what they wrote with a partner, and then calls on a few students to share with the class.

4. If a student does not mention it, the teacher points out that Feynman's statement can mean we understand best what we explain or teach to others, and provides a short example from his or her own life. The teacher tells students they are going to get a chance to be teachers. They will be able to pick their topics (though the teacher might want to narrow it down to something related to what the class has learned in the past three months). But first, the teacher explains, the class is going to learn the qualities of an effective lesson. By doing so, the teacher says, students will also be able to hold the teacher accountable for preparing good lessons.

5. The teacher explains that he or she is going to distribute eight pages from a book ("Question 8" from *Helping Students Motivate Themselves*) and

that the class is going to discuss it in a "jigsaw" fashion. *Jigsaw* describes a process where, for example, students are given different portions of the same article or different articles entirely and then have to become experts on their part and make a presentation to others.

Sixteen elements of an effective lesson are reviewed, along with an introduction. Depending on how many students are in the class, the teacher might want to assign each student two sections for a total of eight separate groups. The teacher assigns each student a number and then writes the numbers on the board next to the sections students will cover. This is the process they will follow:

First, students read their assigned sections. They are to write a short summary of each one, underline a quote they like from each section, and list at least one question about it. They will have ten minutes to do this activity.

Second, they will meet with all the other students who were assigned their sections. They will share what they wrote and then, as a group, complete a graphic organizer (Figure 1.2) the teacher will give them. (The teacher might or might not want to consider creating a model using one of the sections in the chapter.) Then they will write this information on a piece of easel paper and be prepared to present it to the class. Their presentation should last no longer than five minutes, and everyone in the group should participate. They will have twenty minutes to create and practice their presentation.

Third, they will take turns presenting to the class. While they are presenting, each student who is listening should be writing questions. The presenting group can choose any one student to ask a question.

NOTE: Another option is to create groups that are composed of one person from each of the numbers. In other words, each group would have a student numbered 1, 2, 3, 4, 5, and 6, and then each student presents what he or she learned to the rest of the group.

6. The teacher then proceeds to have the class follow this three-part process. It is likely only two or three groups will have time to present. At the end of the class, the teacher explains that the presentations will continue the next day.

Second Day:

1. The teacher does a quick review of the previous day and continues with student presentations and questions.

2. After all presentations are complete, the teacher asks students: "Which of the instructional strategies do you think is most important?" They are to write one paragraph using the ABC format (Answer the question; Back it up with a quote or other evidence; make a Connection to an experience or another text). See Chapter 6 in this book for an example. After five to seven minutes, students

can do a quick "pair-share," and then the teacher can call on some students to share with the class. This entire activity should not take more than fifteen minutes. However, if this is the first time students have done an ABC paragraph, the teacher should take an extra five minutes to explain and model it.

3. The teacher now explains that students will work in pairs over the next two days to choose a topic of interest that is related to what the class has studied during the past three months; research the topic further online; prepare a plan for a lesson that should last ten to fifteen minutes; and then teach it to a small group. Teachers can offer students a collection of websites and books related to what has been studied in addition to a list of topic ideas to help students get started. The teacher then uses Figure 1.3 to complete a model lesson plan on the overhead. The teacher explains that students should decide on their partners and, ideally, their topics, by the end of this class period. Students need to be told that their topic is subject to teacher approval. They will have tomorrow to research in the computer lab and then half of the following day to finalize and practice their lessons. Students will begin teaching their lessons on the fourth day and finish them on the fifth day.

4. The teacher asks students to identify their partners and gives a lesson plan sheet to each pair of students. He or she asks them to write their names and the topic before the end of class. If there is extra time, students can begin to complete the list of things they want their students to get out of the lesson.

5. Teacher collects lesson plan sheets and reviews them after class, making notes on what to say to students to help them focus their lesson plans.

Third Day:

1. Teacher returns the lesson plan sheets to students and brings the class to the computer lab. The teacher reminds students to also bring the entire chapter from *Helping Students Motivate Themselves,* even though they were responsible for presenting a only small part of it. They will be able to refer back to it in their lesson planning. The teacher explains that he or she will have to approve each lesson plan by signing it.

2. The teacher circulates among students while they are online, talking with them about their lesson plans.

3. A few minutes before class ends, the teacher explains that students will have the first half of class the next day to prepare and practice their lesson plan. At that point, the teacher will assign small groups, with three pairs of students in each group; each pair will teach their lesson to the other four students in the group. There should be enough time for one or two pairs to teach before the end of that class period, and the remaining pair(s) can finish the following day.

Fourth Day:

1. Students are given the first half of the first period to prepare and practice their lesson.

2. At the midpoint of class, the teacher reviews Figure 1.4 and Figure 1.5. The teacher explains that at the end of each lesson, the "teachers" will complete one copy of the teacher self-evaluation and the "students" will complete one copy of the student evaluation. The teacher might want to model completing each form on the overhead. Students will have no more than five minutes to complete them and one minute to share them with the other group, and turn both in to the teacher.

3. The teacher identifies the order in which pairs will present, based on lesson topics and behavioral interaction.

4. Students begin to teach lessons. Ideally, two pairs will complete their lessons by the end of the period, and the last one will finish on the following day. However, if necessary, two pairs can complete their lessons on the following day.

Fifth Day:

1. The teacher asks students to get into their groups and complete teaching their lessons. Then the teacher collects the group evaluation forms.

2. The teacher asks students to divide a paper into two columns. In one column they should list what they found to be the hardest things about teaching. In the other column they should list what they thought were the easiest things. After a few minutes, the teacher asks students to turn their paper over and divide that side into two columns. In one column they should list what they did when they were in the student role, and what their "students" did, to make it a better learning experience. In the other column, students should list things they did as students that weren't helpful, or additional good things they could have done.

3. After a few minutes, the teacher should divide students into groups of three or four to verbally share their responses quickly. Then the teacher could bring the class together and ask a few students to share.

4. The teacher asks students to respond to this question using the ABC format: "What was the most important thing you learned about teaching?" Prior to asking students to begin writing, however, the teacher will show one or two good examples of an ABC paragraph written by students on the second day. Students are given five minutes to write their answers, and are then asked to share with a partner who was not in their teaching/learning group. The teacher can be circulating during this process to see what students have written and can call on a few of them to share with the class.

5. The teacher asks students to write anonymous responses to three questions posted on the overhead: What did you like best about this activity? How could this activity be improved? How would you rate this activity between a one and a five, with one being the worst and five being the best? The teacher asks a student to collect the responses.

Assessment

1. The lesson plans, evaluations, and two ABC paragraphs should provide easily assessable student products.

2. If desired, teachers could develop their own for use with this activity. See "The Best Rubric Sites (And A Beginning Discussion About Their Use)" (www.larryferlazzo.edublogs.org/2010/09/18/the-best-rubric-sites-and-a-beginning-discussion-about-their-use) for multiple free online tools for creating rubrics.

Possible Extensions

- Student lessons could be videotaped and posted on a class blog for later viewing by students and parents. See "The Best Teacher Resources For Online Student Safety & Legal Issues" (www.larryferlazzo.edublogs.org/2009/08/10/the-best-teacher-resources-for-online-student-safety-legal-issues) for permission sheets to be signed by parents and guardians to allowing posting of student work.

- Students could be asked to write a modified ABC paragraph responding to other questions, such as: "What is the most important thing you learned about being a student, and how could you apply that knowledge in class?"

- Students could summarize their ABC paragraphs into posters that would hang on classroom walls and serve as reminders for the rest of the year. The teacher could refer to them periodically.

- The teacher could ask students which of the instructional strategies they would like him or her to use more of in lessons and why.

- As mentioned earlier in the Ed Tech box on FedEx Days, students could be invited to create lessons on any topics they wish, rather than just topics related to something previously studied in class.

Figure 1.2 Elements of a Successful Lesson: Jigsaw Project

You will be working with a partner to read about what makes a lesson successful in preparation for the teaching you will do next week.

Directions:

1. Please read your sections carefully (you may take turns reading aloud) and highlight important words/phrases.

2. Create a poster on a piece of white paper for each of the elements you read about with the following parts:

> ## Element
>
> Write one sentence explaining *what it is.*
>
> Write one sentence explaining *why it is important.*
>
> Give an *example.*
>
> Draw a *sketch* to show your understanding of this element.

3. Be prepared to share your posters with the class.

Figure 1.3 Lesson Plan

Names of group members: _____

_____

Topic you will be teaching: _____

What are three key things you want students to get out of your lesson?

1. _____

2. _____

3. _____

What materials, if any, do you need duplicated? _____

_____

Did you e-mail the links to any materials you want duplicated, or give a
hard copy, to your teacher, including your names and how many copies you
needed?   ☐ Yes   ☐ No

Do you need to use a computer during your lesson?   ☐ Yes   ☐ No

If so, for how long? _____

You must use between three and six of the eleven qualities of an effective lesson
(more is great). Check which ones you are going to use below. On the back of
this sheet, please explain your plan for each one and why you decided to use it.

- ☐ Strategic Introduction (in your explanation, please specify which
  elements of the strategic introduction you are going to use)
- ☐ Movement
- ☐ Choices
- ☐ Minimize Lecture and Emphasize Cooperative Learning
- ☐ Wait Time
- ☐ Visuals
- ☐ Explicit Pattern Seeking
- ☐ Fun
- ☐ Feedback
- ☐ Formative Assessment
- ☐ Reflections, Review, Summarize

How long will your lesson take (ideally, it should be less than 15 minutes)? ____

On the back of this sheet, below your explanations of each lesson quality, write
a timed agenda listing the name of each person responsible for each part.

How many times did you practice the entire lesson? _____

Figure 1.4   Lesson Self-Evaluation for Teachers
(those teaching the lesson complete this form as a group)

Names of teachers _____

Names of students _____

Topic _____

Review your lesson plan.

Do you think your students got the three things you wanted them to get out of the lesson? If yes, why? If no, why not?

Grade your group on each of the lesson plan qualities. Please write at least one sentence for each justifying your grade.

Strategic Introduction _____

_____

Movement _____

_____

Choices _____

_____

Minimize Lecture and Emphasize Cooperative Learning _____

_____

Wait Time _____

_____

Visuals _____

_____

Explicit Pattern Seeking_____

_____

Fun _____

_____

Feedback _____

_____

Formative Assessment _____

_____

Reflections, Review, Summarize _____

_____

What do you think was the best part of the lesson, and why do you think it was the best?

What could you have improved in the lesson?

What did you learn about teaching?

Figure 1.5 Lesson Evaluation for Students
(students being taught complete this form as a group)

Names of teachers _____
Names of students _____
Topic _____

What are the three main things you got out of the lesson?_____
_____
_____

Grade your group on each of the lesson plan qualities. Please write at least one
sentence for each justifying your grade

Strategic Introduction _____
_____

Movement _____
_____

Choices _____
_____

Minimize Lecture and Emphasize Cooperative Learning _____
_____

Wait Time _____
_____

Visuals _____
_____

Explicit Pattern Seeking_____
_____

Fun _____
_____

Feedback _____
_____

Formative Assessment _____
_____

Reflections, Review, Summarize _____
_____

What do you think was the best part of the lesson, and why do you think it was the best?

What could you have improved in the lesson?

Was your group composed of students who took the lesson seriously? If not, what could
you have done differently?

Chapter 2

What Can You Do

to Help Students Feel More Positive About School and Learning?

Sometimes my students are so negative! They're in a bad mood, they whine about everything, and it spreads so quickly. I try to be positive and upbeat, but on some days it doesn't seem to make any difference ...

Studies show that feeling positive emotions enhances attention and higher-order thinking skills ("How We Feel," 2009) as well as encourages perseverance (Kotz, 2012). These are just a few of the many reasons teachers need to consider this chapter's question.

A community organizing adage says that when organizers are having a bad day, all they can do is focus on doing good organizing and it will eventually get better.

A similar perspective can be applied to teaching. Some days, one or two or all of your students are not going to be in a positive frame of mind—and generally it will have nothing to do with anything you did. Issues around their family, friends, boyfriends or girlfriends, etc., can prey on student minds, and, just as studies have shown that self-control and positive behavior can be contagious (Lehrer, 2010), most teachers know that the same thing can be true with negativity.

All we can do at that point is focus on good teaching, and things will eventually get better. Good teaching includes many of the ideas discussed in this book, particularly the ones in the motivation section. This chapter, though, will share some specific ideas on how to increase the odds of moving students from feeling negative about school and academic learning to feeling more positive, and will include immediate approaches, setting-the-stage ideas, two mini-lessons, and two full lesson plans.

There are psychological and physiological challenges that can make helping students *want* to develop more positive feelings an uphill battle. And this reinforces why it is even more essential that teachers be proactive about implementing a positive approach. As well-known professor, author, and researcher Roy Baumeister points out, extensive research finds that: "bad emotions … and bad feedback have more impact than good ones" (Tugend, 2012).

The brain appears to process negative information more thoroughly, and the emotions created tend to last longer. This appears to have an evolutionary basis—our ancestors were probably more likely to survive by being particularly attuned to bad things and therefore more likely to pass on their genes (Tugend, 2012).

The progress principle was mentioned in Chapter 1, and the researcher who identified this concept, Harvard professor Teresa M. Amabile, discussed in *The New York Times* how the power of negativity can directly impact the workplace (and it doesn't seem to be too much of a stretch to expect similar consequences in the classroom):

> "We found that of all the events that could make for a great day
> at work, the most important was making progress on meaningful
> work—even a small step forward," said Professor Amabile …. "A
> setback, on the other hand, meant the employee felt blocked in some
> way from making such progress. Setbacks stood out on the worst
> days at work." (Tugend, 2012, para. 17)

After analyzing some 12,000 diary entries, Amabile said she found that the negative effect of a setback at work on happiness was more than twice as strong as the positive effect of an event that signaled progress. And the power of a setback to increase frustration is more than three times as strong as the power of progress to decrease frustration (Tugend, 2012).

Before we move on to specifics about what this might mean for our students, an overarching idea to keep in mind is that a key tool in teaching is one's ear—more so than one's mouth. This next story will demonstrate how that belief can dramatically increase the chances that our students will remain positive:

In the late 19th century, William Ewart Gladstone had been the premier of England for six years. He was followed by another statesman, Benjamin Disraeli.

This is how the queen of England described the relationship she had with them: "When I left the dining room after sitting next to Mr. Gladstone, I thought he was the cleverest man in England," she said. "But after sitting next to Mr. Disraeli, I thought I was the cleverest woman in England" (Aldous, 2007).

> Trying to be like Mr. Disraeli probably was in that situation—listening, being relational, building on the other person's interest,

demonstrating empathy and curiosity—will go a long way toward helping our students have a more positive outlook.

Immediate Responses

Building Relationships

Building supportive teacher-student relationships is important for numerous reasons, including to help teachers learn about the dreams and hopes of their students. They can then use that knowledge to help connect lessons to students' interests and goals. In researcher John Hattie's recent review of 800 meta-analyses of factors influencing student achievement, he finds that the quality of these relationships ranks 12th—out of 138 (Hattie, 2012, p. 251)!

Education researcher Robert Marzano sums it up simply by saying, "If the relationship between the teacher and the students is good, then everything else that occurs in the classroom seems to be enhanced" (Marzano, 2007, p. 150).

Giving Criticism

Maintaining a positive atmosphere in the classroom does not mean making it a constructive criticism–free zone. Obviously, we all need helpful critique in order to grow.

The question is: How can we offer constructive criticism in a way that supports creating a positive classroom atmosphere?

One way is to always keep "the Losada line" in mind. Psychologist Marcial Losada found that it was necessary to have a ratio of three positive interactions for every critical one in order to develop and maintain a healthy team (McInnes, 2011).

A second way is to be strategic about how to deliver criticism. A popular method is the "criticism sandwich": beginning with a compliment, giving a critique, and then ending with another compliment. There has been some criticism (no pun intended) of this method because of what was mentioned earlier in this chapter—since the brain takes more cognitive power to process negative remarks and remembers them more easily, it may forget the preceding praise. Professor Clifford Nass of Stanford instead recommends that one leads with the criticism and then follow with extensive praise (Tugend, 2012).

Professor Nass's research notwithstanding, I personally have found the criticism sandwich more effective with most students, but teachers might want to try both ways to see which works best for their students.

Finally, research suggests that because of the processing time criticism requires, it is best to give only one critical comment at a time (Tugend, 2012).

Starting the Day Off Well

Nobel laureate Daniel Kahneman has identified the importance of "good endings"—what happens at the end of events tends to be what we remember, and what we use to make decisions in the future (Kahneman, 2010).

Beginnings, though, also have an important role.

Researchers have found evidence supporting the wisdom behind the old adage of "starting your day off on the right foot." Scientists examined call center employees, but it appears the lessons could easily apply to students (or just about anyone). They concluded that if you started the day in a positive mood, then you were likely to continue that way. And it found the opposite to be the case, too. Here is what one of the study's authors said:

> The results showed that when employees started the day in a good mood, they tended to rate customers more positively through the day. They also tended to feel more positively themselves as the day progressed.
>
> "Starting off at work wearing rose-colored glasses—or gray glasses—shapes the way we perceive events the rest of the day," Wilk said. ("Got Up on the Wrong Side," 2011)

The way teachers start off the day with their students can obviously have a major effect on how the students will feel for the rest of the day. A greeting with a smile, an engaging lesson, a helpful attitude—these are all important all the time, but especially so at the beginning of the school day.

Being Courteous

Researchers, and many of our own personal experiences, have found that saying *please* (Rathvon, 2008) and *thank you* (Sutton, 2008) can have many positive effects.

The same holds true for *I'm sorry*. Teachers are just humans, and we make plenty of mistakes. There is no reason why we should not apologize for them when we do. In fact, adults saying *I'm sorry* can have a particularly powerful positive effect on children's emotions. One study that identified this kind of impact with young people concluded:

> Knowing that the other person agrees that it was the wrong thing to do reaffirms our view of the world as just and predictable, since the other's sadness tells us that people in general don't do things like this, because after all, it was the wrong thing to do. (Lopez-Duran, 2009, para. 18)

It is possible that many of our students often experience adults doing "things like this" without hearing any kind of apology, so it is particularly important that teachers model this kind of behavior.

But just saying the two words *I'm sorry* may not be enough.

A medical journal in Scotland recommends using a "regret, reason, and remedy" formula (Armstrong, 2009). For example, one day I was a bit sharp with two students who were paired up to do work in my English class, but who were instead just sitting there while everyone else in class was focusing on the task at hand. A few minutes later I came back to them and simply said, "I'm sorry I barked at you earlier. You're both excellent students, and I was frustrated that you weren't doing what I had asked you to do. I could have said so in a better way, and I'll try to show more patience in the future." They clearly refocused much more energy on the work after they heard my detailed apology.

Writing Gratitude Letters

A substantial amount of research shows that students who regularly write down the things they are grateful for experience a more positive sense of well-being, better sleep, and greater levels of energy. Doing it daily has had the best results, but even writing weekly can have positive effects ("Want to Be Happier?" 2008). In fact, one study found that levels of gratitude could be used to accurately predict "higher grade point average, life satisfaction, social integration, and absorption, as well as lower envy and depression" ("What Happens When You Evaluate Students," 2010).

Having students take a minute to jot down what they are grateful for, and then having them share with a partner during a regular weekly reflection time or when you have a few extra minutes at the end of a lesson might be a good use of time. (Perhaps it could alternate with sharing positive events—see the next section.) A teacher could introduce this practice with the following mini-lesson:

Mini-Lesson: Gratitude

1. Teacher writes the word *gratitude* on the overhead, says it, and then asks students to take a few seconds to think about what it means. The teacher then asks students to share their thoughts with a partner, and asks for a few to share with the class. The teacher then writes a definition on the overhead.

2. The teacher explains that he or she is going to periodically ask students to write briefly about things that they are grateful for, and

that he or she is going to share a read aloud that explains why. The teacher asks students to read along silently as he or she puts Figure 2.1 on the overhead. (The teacher may or may not want to distribute copies afterward to the class).

3. The teacher says he or she is going to ask students to write two things they are grateful for and why. Then the teacher writes an example on the overhead.

4. Students are given five minutes to write, then are asked to share with a partner. The teacher then asks a few students he or she had identified while circulating through the classroom to share with the class.

5. The teacher collects student papers. After reviewing them later in the day, he or she might return them with specific suggestions that students share what they wrote with a parent, a friend, a teacher—particularly if they focused on one of them in their paper. The teacher might want to follow up with the student afterward to see what happened.

In addition, having students compose a gratitude letter to someone could help refine their writing skills. (The letter doesn't necessarily have to be sent.) For example, students could write to important people in their lives using the speech Nelson Mandela gave upon his release from prison as a model (Halsall, 1997). The first portion of that speech is all about the idea of gratitude.

Figure 2.1   Gratitude Read-Aloud

"Adults who frequently feel grateful have more energy, more optimism, more social connections and more happiness than those who do not, according to studies conducted over the past decade. They're also less likely to be depressed, envious, greedy or alcoholics. They earn more money, sleep more soundly, exercise more regularly and have greater resistance to viral infections.

"Now, researchers are finding that gratitude brings similar benefits in children and adolescents. Kids who feel and act grateful tend to be less materialistic, get better grades, set higher goals, complain of fewer headaches and stomach aches and feel more satisfied with their friends, families and schools than those who don't, studies show."

Source: Beck (2010, November 23)

Talking About Positive Events in Students' Lives

As part of a regular weekly reflection, perhaps each Friday, students could write briefly about one or two good things that happened to them during the week and why they happened (identifying those reasons can help students see common actions they can do more often to increase the quality and quantity of positive events in their lives). Students can then verbally share what they wrote with other students. Studies have shown that sharing positive events with others creates a more trusting and supportive environment, especially if people react positively to what is shared ("What's an Easy Way to Strengthen," 2010). Students sharing their experiences with a partner, and then having the listener show interest by asking questions, could have a similar effect. A teacher could introduce this practice with the following mini-lesson:

Mini-Lesson: Optimism

1. The teacher writes the words *optimism* and *pessimism* on the whiteboard. He or she says the words, and asks students to take a few seconds to think if they know what they mean. He or she then asks students to share with a partner and has some students share with the class. The teacher then writes the words *optimist* and *pessimist* and explains that that those words describe people who have feelings of optimism or pessimism. He or she also explains that a person doesn't necessarily have to be one or the other, but can be somewhere in between.

2. The teacher explains that he or she is going to periodically ask students to write about positive events that occur in their lives and share them. He or she then presents a short read-aloud (Figure 2.2, page 36) on the overhead that explains how this writing is connected to optimism. The teachers says he or she would like students to read along silently. After reading, he or she shares an example of a time when something good came out of something bad that happened in his or her life. (The teacher may want to distribute copies of the read-aloud afterward to students.)

3. The teacher explains that students are going to try the activity for the first time: writing about two positive things that happened to them in the past week and what they might have done to contribute to those things happening. The teacher models doing it on the overhead. He or she explains that today, students will also write a third thing—about a time when something good came out of something bad that happened in their lives. The teacher can refer back to his or her example. Students are given five minutes to write.

Figure 2.2 Optimism Read-Aloud

"Optimism is the belief that good things will happen to you and that negative events are temporary setbacks to be overcome" (Mayo Clinic staff, 2011).

Research shows that people who are optimists live longer, are healthier, have less stress in their lives, and are happier.

Optimists tend to confront problems and look for something good to come from them. In other words, they look at what they can they learn from difficult situations so they can become better people.

What can people do to become more optimistic?

They can write regularly about positive things that happen to them.

They can use "self-talk." For example, instead of thinking to themselves, "I can't do this because I've never done this before," they can tell themselves, "This is an opportunity to learn something new."

They can surround themselves with positive people.

Sources: Mayo Clinic staff (2011) & Brody (2012, May 21)

4. Teacher asks students to share verbally with a partner what they wrote and circulates through the classroom to identify students who will share with the class (for sensitive topics, the teacher should ask students if they feel comfortable sharing).

5. Teacher asks a few students to share with the class and collects students' papers.

Setting the Stage

Visualization

In the past, I had very limited success at using visualization and guided imagery in my own life, so I have been reluctant to encourage others to try it.

Until a few years ago.

That year, I had a particularly challenging student who had a number of self-control issues and typically had a negative outlook each day. In fact, he is the only student I've had that other students came and complained to me about. He repeatedly told me he knew he needed to make changes and that he wanted to—and I was convinced he was sincere—but nothing we tried worked.

As a last resort, I suggested that he go outside to read his book during our silent reading time (which began each class) and, before he started to read, close his eyes for a couple of minutes and see himself acting as the student he wanted to be—cooperative, positive, friendly, and focused, instead of always reacting to provocations. He was willing to give it a try, and it had an immediate positive effect. It produced much better results than anything else we had tried. We continued with this daily practice for the rest of the school year and, even though he was not the perfect student, he handled himself much, much better.

Subsequently, Jim Peterson, a talented administrator at our school who also happens to be a behavioral therapist and a clinical hypnotherapist, suggested I try a similar technique with the rest of my students. The first full lesson plan in this chapter shares how this can be introduced and continued on an ongoing basis for a minute each day. (For a video of the lesson and a link to Peterson's website, go to www.larryferlazzo.edublogs. org/2010/01/27/results-from-having-ell-students-visualize-success.)

Research has shown visualizing success can be effective in many ways, including by increasing confidence (Schlosberg, 1998) and reducing stress (Shore, 2010), both attributes that can be helpful in developing a positive attitude. Visualization is perhaps most famously used by athletes to improve their performance and has been found to be particularly successful in activities where a high degree of cognitive skills is required (Kosslyn & Moulton, 2008, p. 39). Extensive research has shown its effectiveness in learning a second language (Dörnyei, n.d.).

In research with my own classes, I have found that students using visualization techniques tend to score approximately 8 percent higher in cloze (fill-in-the-gap passages to measure reading comprehension and vocabulary development) assessments. In addition, having students use one minute as quiet time near the beginning of class—whether or not they are actually using it to visualize—can have a calming and positive effect on the classroom atmosphere.

Modeling

One of the biggest lessons teachers often learn is the importance of modeling for students before they are expected to do a particular assignment—writing, reading strategies, etc. Teacher modeling seems to make a huge difference and is recommended by many researchers, including Robert Marzano (Holt McDougal Literature for Texas, n.d.).

Modeling appropriate behavior can also be important. In fact, it appears that students just witnessing positive behavior on video can have an impact.

One study showed that students seeing people performing acts of kindness were more likely to perform altruistic acts themselves (Nauert, 2010).

However, adult modeling might have somewhat limited success. As studies have shown, peer behavior functions as a more effective model for young people (Berten, 2008).

The second full lesson plan in this chapter tries to combine the importance of modeling, peer influence, and the results from the study about seeing positive behavior on video. In this lesson plan, teachers help students identify specific areas of positive classroom behavior—for example, working in a small group and eliciting participation from everybody, along with other examples included in this book—and have student groups create short videos of themselves modeling a behavior of their choice. Certainly, humor can be an element. The plan can also be modified to have students perform live in the classroom.

Visualization Lesson Plan

Instructional Objectives for Students:

- Learn about visualization techniques and how to apply them.

- Practice visualizing for success.

- Practice reading strategies.

Duration: Thirty minutes, plus one minute each day (Note: This lesson is best done after students have identified goals. See, for example, the lesson plans in Chapter 6.)

Materials:

- Student copies of Figure 2.3, page 43

- Computer projector and Internet access

- Document camera or overhead projector

Common Core English Language Arts Standards

Reading: Determine central ideas or themes of a text and analyze their development; summarize the key supporting details and ideas.

Writing: Produce clear and coherent writing in which the development, organization, and style are appropriate to task, purpose, and audience.

Speaking and Listening: Prepare for and participate effectively in a range of conversations and collaborations with diverse partners, building on others' ideas and expressing their own clearly and persuasively.

Language:

- Demonstrate command of the conventions of standard English grammar and usage when writing or speaking.

- Demonstrate command of the conventions of standard English capitalization, punctuation, and spelling when writing.

Procedure

First Day:

1. Teacher asks all students to stand and spread out. They should be able to stretch their arms in all directions without touching anyone or anything. The teacher then asks all students to hold out one arm straight in front of them (keeping the other one down by their side). Then, he or she asks the students to keep their arm outstretched and straight and, keeping their eyes looking forward, move their arm to the back perpendicular to their body as far as possible without straining (the teacher should be modeling the procedure). He or she then asks the students to keep their arm in that location and to look and remember where their arm was pointing to when it reached its limit. NOTE: A video of this portion of the lesson can be found at http://larryferlazzo.edublogs.org/2010/01/27/results-from-having-ell-students-visualize-success/

2. Then, the teacher will ask students to close their eyes and mentally visualize (without doing the physical movement) doing the same thing several times—stretching as far as they can. They should start off imagining it happening slowly and then repeat it several times faster. Each time they should see themselves moving their arm from the front to as far back as it can go, while keeping it perpendicular to the rest of their body. Students should repeat visualizing (but not physically doing) this movement for about two minutes.

3. Next, the teacher should ask students to open their eyes and physically put their arm in front of them, and then physically move it to the back as far as they can while looking forward. They should remember how far they stretched the first time, and then look at how far they are stretching now. Most should see that they can easily stretch their arm much farther this time.

4. The teacher explains that this is called visualizing success. The idea is that by repeating actions in our minds, it is easier to do them in real life. The teacher says students are going to learn more about visualizing today, and how they can use it to help themselves achieve their goals—whether to become a better student, a more positive person, a better public speaker, etc.

5. The teacher asks students to sit down and explains that he or she is going to distribute a one-page sheet about visualizing success (Figure 2.3). The teacher asks students to get with a partner and take turns reading each section to each other. After reading each section, they are to either draw a picture or make a connection—in writing—to a personal experience, something else they have read, or a movie they have seen. The teacher circulates through the room and identifies students to call on during class discussion.

6. After five minutes, the teacher reads each section on the sheet and asks certain students to share what they wrote or drew. If the teacher has a document camera, the students can bring their drawings to the front.

7. Next, the teacher shares one or two Internet videos showing athletes visualizing or talking about visualizing. Many examples can be found at "The Best Videos To Help Students Visualize Success" (www.larryferlazzo.edublogs.org/2012/11/05/the-best-videos-to-help-students-visualize-success). Teachers can learn ways to use YouTube videos at school here: "The Best Ways To Access Educational YouTube Videos At School" (www.larryferlazzo.edublogs.org/2008/12/20/the-best-ways-to-access-educational-youtube-videos-in-school) if the site itself is blocked.

8. The teacher then explains that students are going to practice visualization. First, they are going to take a minute to think about a goal they want to achieve (ideally, the class is using some of the goal-setting tips described in Chapter 1). For example, a student might have a goal of showing more patience. He or she could visualize themselves not reacting in a situation where they might typically show impatience. Or a student who has not been regularly doing homework might visualize sitting down and doing it, and not getting distracted by television. Then, the teacher asks everyone to close their eyes and silently see themselves achieving their goals. The teacher asks students to stop after one minute.

9. The teacher explains that the class is going to do this exercise for one minute each day. Sometimes it will be before a major lesson, like writing an essay, and the teacher might ask students to see themselves as great writers and see people complimenting them on their writing. Other times, the teacher might ask them to see themselves being great readers. And, other times, students might be asked just to see themselves achieving any goals they have identified. The teacher also explains that people will not be required to visualize—if they prefer they can just relax, with their eyes open or closed. But everyone will need to be silent and not doing anything distracting. The teacher encourages students to participate, though, reminding students that the technique helps, as they learned today.

10. The teacher does the assessment with students.

Each Day Thereafter:

1. The teacher will say something like this to students: "Please put down your pencils, close your eyes, and see yourself achieving one of your goals. It is fine if you do not want to visualize—just sit with your eyes closed or open, with your head up or down, and relax. Please do make any noise."

2. Periodically, the teacher can ask students to write down if they are visualizing or not, and what they see if they are. The teacher should emphasize that he or she would like people to be honest, and that there is not penalty for not visualizing.

Assessment

- The teacher writes two questions on the board for students to answer: "What was the most important or most interesting thing you learned in this lesson?" and "When you visualized success, what did you see?"

- If desired, the teacher could also have students respond to the first question using the ABC format explained in Chapter 6.

- If the teacher feels a more involved assessment is necessary, he or she can develop a simple rubric appropriate for the classroom situation. Free online resources to both find existing rubrics and to create new ones can be found at "The Best Rubric Sites (And A Beginning Discussion About Their Use)" (www.larryferlazzo.edublogs.org/2010/09/18/ the-best-rubric-sites-and-a-beginning-discussion-about-their-use).

Possible Extensions

- The teacher can do his or her own research and design assessments to compare the improvement of students doing the visualizing with those who are not. This research can compare students within one class or compare classes.

- Students can teach what they have learned about visualization techniques and how they can be useful to another class.

Ed Tech
Drawing Tools

Students could periodically use a simple online application like Flashpaint (www.flashpaint.com) to draw what they are visualizing, as well as describing it in writing. Students could post links to these drawings and descriptions on a class blog or other website, and other students could view and comment on them. Or, they could be shown in the classroom on a computer projector. Many other easy online drawing tools can be found at "The Best Art Websites For Learning English" (www.larryferlazzo.edublogs. org/2008/02/01/the-best-art-websites-for-learning-english).

Figure 2.3   Visualizing Success

- In a famous experiment, students were asked to hit a golf ball into a hole, and their scores were recorded. Then, some were told to visualize putting the ball into the hole, and others were told to visualize putting the ball right next to the hole. The people who visualized positively scored more than 30 percent higher than they did the first time, and those who visualized negatively scored 21 percent lower.

- Studies have shown that athletes surgeons, and airline pilots, among many others, can use visualization to measurably improve their performance. (In one study, 80 percent of 63 world-class athletes said they used visualization.)

- Mental imagery (visualization) has been found by a committee of the National Academy of Sciences to be an effective performance-enhancing activity.

Source: Kosslyn & Moulton (2008)

How the Navy SEALs Increased Passing Rates

Three-quarters of the people in the Navy SEALs training program were failing, and its leaders were concerned they were losing good recruits. They did not want to make the training program less rigorous, however.

They were able to increase passing rates by teaching recruits to do four things:

- Set short-term goals
- Visualize themselves succeeding in their activities
- Speak to themselves positively
- Monitor their breathing when they were feeling stressed

Source: Akil (2009, November 9)

Modeling Positive Behavior Lesson Plan

Instructional Objectives for Students:

- Work in small groups to identify a positive behavior they want to model through a short skit.

- Create a video of their skit for use during the year and for online display, if desired.

Duration: Two to three sixty-minute class periods, depending upon whether the skits are videotaped or just performed live

Materials:

- Student copies of a storyboard (a page or pages divided into boxes representing scenes in a story). There are many available online, including at "The Best Digital (& Nondigital) Storytelling Resources" (www.larryferlazzo. edublogs.org/2009/04/15/the-best-digital-storytelling-resources).

- A computer projector and access to the Internet for showing instructional videos on manners hosted on the Internet. Searching for videos with the phrase "manners etiquette 1950s" will result in numerous choices.

- A video camera or smartphone (and tripod) and computer access for editing if part of the lesson will be to make a video. The other option is to have students perform the skit without taping it.

- Index cards for students to write their "script notes"

- Between 100 and 150 copies of Figure 2.4, page 48

Common Core English Language Arts Standards

Writing: Produce clear and coherent writing in which the development, organization, and style are appropriate to task, purpose, and audience.

Speaking and Listening:

- Prepare for and participate effectively in a range of conversations and collaborations with diverse partners, building on others' ideas and expressing their own clearly and persuasively.

- Present information, findings, and supporting evidence such that listeners can follow the line of reasoning and the organization, development, and style are appropriate to task, purpose, and audience.

- Make strategic use of digital media and visual displays of data to express information and enhance understanding of presentations.

- Adapt speech to a variety of contexts and communicative tasks, demonstrating command of formal English when indicated or appropriate.

Language:

- Demonstrate command of the conventions of standard English grammar and usage when writing or speaking.

- Demonstrate command of the conventions of standard English capitalization, punctuation, and spelling when writing.

Procedure

First Day:

1. The teacher explains the class is going to watch a short video today. He or she picks one of the funnier films from the 1950s showing how to behave at the dinner table (or something similar).

2. The teacher says students might be wondering why he or she showed that movie and goes on to say that students are going to make their own version of a video modeling appropriate behavior. Small groups will pick a classroom behavior to model, perform a short skit (with humor or without), and then videotape it to periodically show to the class. If they want, they can make two short skits, one showing how not to behave and a second showing appropriate positive behavior. The entire presentation should not be more than three or four minutes long.

3. The teacher lists some examples students could model (ideally, this lesson occurs after the teacher has taught other lessons in this book):

   o Taking personal responsibility instead of blaming others for their mistakes

   o Being a community of learners and not just a classroom of students

   o Being polite

   o Encouraging everyone to talk in a small group and neither monopolizing the conversation nor staying silent

   o Praising effort instead of intelligence

   The teacher can ask for other ideas from students. He then tells students they will work in groups of three to plan and perform the skit.

4. The teacher explains that he or she will give students five minutes to divide into small groups and write down three topics they might want to act out. They should rank them 1, 2, or 3 in order of preference. At the end of that time, they should hand in those sheets to the teacher for review, and the teacher will decide who will use which topic. Two groups can perform the same topic, but three might be too much repetition. The teacher explains that after each group has their topic, he or she will lay out the process students will be using to make the skit.

5. After the topics are decided, the teacher shows a storyboard on the document camera or overhead projector. He or she can choose from various examples, but it should probably have no fewer than 10 boxes with space for text and illustrations. The teacher can model what would go in one or two boxes. The first one can be the introduction, and if groups are doing two skits (one showing the wrong way to behave, the other showing the right way), there should be a transition.

6. The teacher explains that students will have the rest of the class period and half of the next to write their storyboard and practice. A simple draft of their storyboard should be done by the end of class. The teacher will start reviewing storyboards with each class by the end of the first day and the beginning of the second day. While he or she is doing that, other groups can continue to refine theirs.

Second Day:

1. The teacher explains that he or she will continue to meet with groups. In addition, each group is going to practice its presentation in front of another group. Students can pick which groups they want to work with, but they should be ones that will be ready to practice at about the same time. Each student in the observing group will complete a feedback form to give to the other group (see Figure 2.4). The teacher reviews the form on the document camera and models appropriately helpful comments, especially for the last two questions. He or she tells the class that after students give another group feedback, they should hand the observation form in to the teacher. The teacher explains that groups will perform in thirty minutes. He or she explains (if skits are being videotaped and edited) that the next day (or on some future day), students will go to the computer lab to edit it. He or she distributes index cards on which students can write their lines.

2. After setting up the video camera or smart phone on a tripod (if skits are being videotaped), the teacher distributes more copies of the feedback form and explains that each student will complete one for each group. After each group performs, and after applause is given, all students are given a minute or two to complete the feedback form, and the teacher collects them.

3. After all groups are done, the teacher gives each group their feedback forms for review.

Third Day (Optional):

If desired, students can use online editing software to refine their presentations. (See www.larryferlazzo.edublogs.org/2010/03/30/not-the-best-but-a-list-of-online-video-editors for suggestions.) Another option is to show the videos as is.

Assessment

- Teachers can collect the peer observation forms for each group.

- If the teacher feels a more involved assessment is necessary, he or she can develop a simple rubric appropriate for the classroom situation. Free online resources to both find existing rubrics and to create new ones can be found at "The Best Rubric Sites (And A Beginning Discussion About Their Use)" (www.larryferlazzo.edublogs.org/2010/09/18/the-best-rubric-sites-and-a-beginning-discussion-about-their-use).

Ed Tech
Post Instructional Videos Online

The teacher, after obtaining written parent permission (see "The Best Teacher Resources For Online Student Safety & Legal Issues," at www.larryferlazzo.edublogs.org/2009/08/10/the-best-teacher-resources-for-online-student-safety-legal-issues), can post the videos online using YouTube or a site like TeacherTube (www.teachertube.com). They then would be easily available to show as reminders during the year, or as models for future classes.

Figure 2.4   Peer Group Observation Sheet

Your Name: _____

Names of students in the group you observed: _____

_____

   1. Did they introduce their topic at the beginning?

   2. Was the main idea communicated by the skit?

   3. Did people speak loudly?

   4. Did they look down at their notecards the whole skit, or did they periodically make eye contact with the other actors?

   5. Did they stick to the three-minute time limit?

   6. Did they try to keep their faces looking toward the audience?

   7. Did they have empty mouths (no gum)?

   8. If students did one skit showing the wrong way to behave and another showing the right way, did they have a transition between the two?

   9. What did you like about the skit?

  10. Is there anything else you can think of that would have made the skit better?

Chapter 3

How Do You

Handle Rudeness in Class?

I've never quite figured out the best response to these kinds of situations:
You're in the middle of a lesson that seems to be going well and are asking students to respond to a question. One gives the wrong answer out loud, and another yells, "You're stupid!" That results in a response from the first student: "At least I'm not fat!" You tell them both to be quiet, but it's hard getting students focused again.
Or you're speaking to the class, or you've asked a student to speak. At the same time, a few other students are whispering to one another. A different student decides to try to be helpful to you and yells, "Shut up! You guys are so immature. ..."
"What do you do?"

Rudeness is not an uncommon experience in our schools. This chapter will share suggestions on how to respond to immediate instances of rudeness, and how to set the stage to preempt acts of rudeness. Three related lesson plans are included. Helping students see that it is in *their* self-interest to be respectful of others can go a long way toward creating a supportive classroom community. It can also be an enormously helpful step toward their developing the "soft" skills (communication, teamwork, etc.) necessary for life success.

Immediate Actions

In the Classroom

When there are instances of chronic rudeness from a student, strategies discussed in Chapter 4 of this book might be appropriate. In other instances, it might be effective to simply say, "I'm not feeling respected right now" or "I don't feel respected when people do (whatever is being done)."

After using the lessons plans included in this chapter with students, other ways to respond include "Is that really how we act in a community of learners?" and "Remember what we learned about rudeness hurting everybody?"

In the vast majority of cases, going over and speaking softly and privately to the offender will elicit a better response than addressing the entire class. However, in cases when there are multiple offenders, a public response in a calm voice might be necessary.

At School but Outside the Classroom

At most schools, teachers don't necessarily know all the students. In the hallways, it might not be uncommon to see students acting or speaking inappropriately with one another. The vast majority of time, this behavior is not an "office-referral-worthy" act of physical violence or threat that requires strong intervention. It might be a curse word said in passing, some quasi-friendly verbal kidding with a bite, or some physical horseplay. It would be easy to just ignore it.

Another possible response is giving a reprimand. That may or may not immediately stop the behavior, but it probably would not enhance any possible future relationship you might have with that student, nor would it probably prevent the student from behaving that way again in a way that wouldn't result in being caught.

A few years ago I came up with a strategy that seems to work well.

When I see or hear inappropriate behavior, I say, in an exaggerated parental tone, "Be niiiiiiicccccceeee." I stretch out the word *nice* when I say it, and my tone is not harsh—just sort of disapproving.

It has almost always resulted in the behavior immediately stopping and a sheepish grin coming to the face of the culprit. In addition, if his or her friends are around, often they will take up the cry: "Yeah, be nice!" Sometimes, I'll even be walking down the hall and a student who I don't know will yell, "I'm being nice, Mr. Ferlazzo!"

I have no way of measuring this technique's long-term effectiveness, but it works in the short term and I feel good about it—certainly a lot better than I would feel if I scolded a student.

A more preventative strategy to take when walking around campus is to just smile at students you don't know. A study found that people who are acknowledged with a smile by a stranger feel more socially connected than people who are ignored (Pappas, 2012). The more we can do to help our students feel connected to the school community, the less likely they are to be rude or disruptive.

Setting the Stage

My primary suggestions on how to set the stage to deal with rudeness are by using three lesson plans. Teaching any or all of these lesson plans provides a reference point for effectively dealing with rudeness when it occurs. Here are brief summaries of each lesson.

Community of Learners

At the beginning of each school year, teachers can do a short lesson contrasting a "community of learners" with a "classroom of students." At the end of the lesson, students vote on which one they want—and it is very likely they will choose a community of learners.

The Latin and Indo-European root words for *community* mean "an exchange shared by all," while *class* or *classroom* is defined in many dictionaries as "a group of students meeting together to be taught." The lesson helps clarify how those two might look different day to day, including on the issue of rudeness.

Rudeness

The rudeness lesson engages students in defining what rudeness is, and shares scientific evidence that suggests its negative effect on the thinking skills of everyone involved—the person being rude, the target of the rudeness, and anybody who witnesses it.

Listening

In the lesson on listening, students will help identify the characteristics of a good listener and a bad one. In addition, they will learn the benefits of being a good listener, backed by scientific evidence.

Community of Learners Lesson Plan

Instructional Objectives for Students: Students will identify the differences between a community of learners and a classroom of students and decide which one they want to be.

Duration: Forty minutes

Materials:

- A document camera/overhead projector or an easel-size sheet of paper

- One copy of Figure 3.1, page 56, as a reminder to the teacher, and another version of the same chart that is blank and ready to be completed by the teacher and students together.

Common Core English Language Arts Standards

Writing:

- Produce clear and coherent writing in which the development, organization, and style are appropriate to task, purpose, and audience.

- Use technology, including the Internet, to produce and publish writing and to interact and collaborate with others.

Speaking and Listening:

- Prepare for and participate effectively in a range of conversations and collaborations with diverse partners, building on others' ideas and expressing their own clearly and persuasively.

- Adapt speech to a variety of contexts and communicative tasks, demonstrating command of formal English when indicated or appropriate.

Language:

- Demonstrate command of the conventions of standard English grammar and usage when writing or speaking.

- Demonstrate command of the conventions of standard English capitalization, punctuation, and spelling when writing.

Procedure

1. The teacher explains that at the beginning of each year he or she likes to have a conversation with students about the two kinds of classes that you can typically find in a school. One is a classroom of students (which, to help illustrate the paradigm, the teacher might want to subtitle "the typical classroom experience") and the other is a community of learners. He or she says that the class is going to spend a few minutes together trying to define the difference between the two, and then decide together which of the two they are going to have this year. It will not be a question of being one or the other all the time but, instead, the class will try to figure out which they are going to be most of the time.

2. The teacher shows a chart similar to Figure 3.1 (the figure itself should only be used by the teacher as a "cheat sheet"). The chart will be blank except for the labels on the top and on the left. The teacher can ask students to take a minute to draw what they think a teacher does and write a sentence describing it. Students can then share with a partner, and the teacher can ask a student or two who wrote something helpful to share his or her drawing and sentence.

   Student responses will probably show the teacher being the source of most knowledge, delivering information to the students and doing most of the talking. The teacher will describe what a teacher does in a community of learners—helps students to teach themselves and other students. A teacher in a community of learners will also learn from students—he or she doesn't know all the answers. A teacher will help connect lessons to the students' lives.

   The teacher can then say this famous quotation, often attributed to William Butler Yeats: "Education is not the filling of a pail but the lighting of a fire." He or she can ask students to do a "think-pair-share" and explain what they think that quote means. After a brief discussion, the teacher can ask in what column on their chart "filling a pail" would go and in which one "lighting of a fire" would be placed.

3. The teacher continues a similar process for the row labeled "Role of Students." The teacher could ask students to take a minute to write what they think the role of students is in a classroom of students and then share what they wrote. They might say students sit and work quietly, and agree with the teacher. In a community of learners students talk and learn from one another, raise questions, and help the teacher refine his or her craft with constructive feedback. They act as cocreators of their learning environment. Students talk as much if not more than the teacher. Things are sometimes little bit messy in a community of learners—the teacher's lesson doesn't always go according to plan.

4. The teacher continues the process as he or she completes the chart. Students might say they are motivated by grades or fear of punishment in a classroom of students. This can be characterized by frequent questions from students about how many points an assignment is worth or wondering if they will get extra credit points for doing something. This is contrasted with the goal and motivating factor in a community of learners, which is to *learn*. Students are motivated to work and behave because they want to learn. The teacher can quote Ralph Waldo Emerson, who said, "The reward of a thing well done is to have done it."

5. The teacher continues the discussion. When a student makes a mistake or does something very well in a classroom of students, there may be ridicule or jealousy. People can be rude to one another. In a community of learners, people are celebrated for taking risks, learning from mistakes, and doing exceptionally good work. Curiosity is encouraged—there is no such thing as a dumb question. People are courteous to one another.

6. The teacher asks students to take a minute to think about other differences between a classroom of students and a community of learners. The teacher asks them to write down their ideas and then, after two or three minutes, has students share with a partner and then with the class. Here are two examples my students have shared in the past:

   o In a *classroom,* "students start a fight and end up hurting each other." In a *community,* "they don't start a fight; they talk it out."

   o In a *classroom,* "the only way to succeed is doing exactly what the teacher says." In a *community,* "you have more than one choice in succeeding."

7. At the end of the discussion, the teacher can dramatically ask students: Which one do you think would be more interesting? Which one do you think would be more fun? Finally, the teacher asks them to write down which kind of classroom they want theirs to be and why. It should be fairly easy for the teacher to make sure that practically all students choose a community of learners. Students share what they wrote with a partner and then take a vote.

8. The teacher announces that he or she will leave the chart on the wall for review during the year to see how the class is doing being a community of learners.

Assessment

- The teacher can turn the chart over so students cannot see it and say, as a test, he or she wants students to write down as many things as they can remember that happen in a community of learners.

- The teacher could ask students to choose which quality in a community of learners they think is most important and why. Students could write a paragraph using the ABC or PQC (make a Point; Quote from the text supporting your point; make a Comment or a connection to your personal experience, another text, or some other knowledge) models that are discussed in other chapters.

Possible Extensions

During the year, the teacher can periodically make the chart a focus of a reflection question.

Ed Tech
Wallwisher

The teacher could bring students to the computer lab and direct them to a specific page on the website Wallwisher (www.wallwisher.com). The teacher could have previously created that page in seconds so that it is ready for student use. At Wallwisher, each student could write one action he or she commits to doing to help support developing a community of learners during the year, and write it on a virtual Post-it note on the Wallwisher page. Each student could also add an image from the Web that represents his or her sentence. The page would then be filled with these commitments from students. All of them could see their wall then, and the teacher could show it periodically during the year, too. If Wallwisher is blocked, many other similar sites can be found at "The Best Online Virtual 'Corkboards' (or 'Bulletin Boards')" (www.larryferlazzo.edublogs. org/2011/03/30/the-best-online-virtual-corkboards-or-bulletin-boards).

Figure 3.1 Compare and Contrast Chart

	Classroom of Students	Community of Learners
Role of teacher	Teaches, lectures, " fills pail," does most of the talking, delivers all information to students	Doesn't know all the answers, helps students to teach themselves and other students, learns from students, "lights the fire"
Role of students	Sit quietly and listen, think the teacher is always right	Talk and learn from one another, help the teacher become better by giving constructive feedback, ask questions, are cocreators of their learning environment
What motivates students	Grades, points, extra credit, fear of punishment	"The reward of a thing well done is to have done it," wanting to learn
What happens when a student makes a mistake or does something well?	Ridicule, jealousy, rudeness, "You're dumb!" "Oooh, Johnny's a brain!"	People are celebrated for taking risks, for learning from mistakes, and for doing exceptionally good work. Students are courteous and want their classmates to be successful. Curiosity is encouraged, and there is no such thing as a dumb question.

Rudeness Lesson Plan

Instructional Objectives for Students:

- Learn what scientific research says are the consequences of rudeness.

- Write a summary of what they have learned.

- Dentify alternate behaviors.

Duration: Thirty minutes

Materials:

- Figure 3.2, page 61 (a read-aloud on rudeness research)

- Document camera or overhead projector

Common Core English Language Arts Standards

Writing:

- Produce clear and coherent writing in which the development, organization, and style are appropriate to task, purpose, and audience.

- Use technology, including the Internet, to produce and publish writing and to interact and collaborate with others.

Speaking and Listening:

- Prepare for and participate effectively in a range of conversations and collaborations with diverse partners, building on others' ideas and expressing their own clearly and persuasively.

- Adapt speech to a variety of contexts and communicative tasks, demonstrating command of formal English when indicated or appropriate.

Language:

- Demonstrate command of the conventions of standard English grammar and usage when writing or speaking.

- Demonstrate command of the conventions of standard English capitalization, punctuation, and spelling when writing.

Procedure

First Day:

1. The teacher writes the word *rudeness* on the whiteboard or overhead, and asks students to take a minute to write a definition of it—without using examples. After a minute, the teacher tells students to share what they wrote with a partner, and then calls on students to share what they wrote with the class. The teacher writes the responses on the board or overheard. The teacher can mention that the word *rude* comes from the Latin word *rudis,* meaning "unlearned."

2. The teacher tells students that the philosopher Eric Hoffer is said to have claimed, "Rudeness is the weak man's imitation of strength." The teacher writes the quote on the board or overhead. Teacher asks students to take a minute or two to write down if they agree or disagree with what he said, and why. After a minute, the teacher tells students to share what they wrote with a partner, and then calls on students to share what they wrote with the class.

3. The teacher then shows these questions on the board or overhead:

   o Think of one or two times when people were rude to you. How did it make you feel?

   o Why do you think people are rude? Have you ever been rude to someone? Why were you rude, and what happened?

4. The teacher explains that students will have five minutes to write answers to these questions. At the end of those five minutes, students share with a partner and then the teacher calls on some to share with the class. Some of the comments will probably relate to emotions.

5. The teacher explains that yes, emotions play a role in rudeness—in both the person being rude and his or her target. The teachers puts Figure 3.2 on the overhead and explains that students should read along silently as he or she reads it aloud. The teacher should note that scientists suspect that, in addition to the negative consequences listed for the people being rude, rude people also suffer many of the negative effects listed for the targets and witnesses of rudeness. The scientists need to do further tests to see if their assumptions are correct. In order to do those tests, people have to admit to being rude, and most people do not want to make that admission.

6. After the teacher reads Figure 3.2, he or she reemphasizes that rudeness hurts the thinking abilities of everybody involved. The teacher can tell the students, "Raise your hand if you want to be less creative, make more mistakes, etc." Assuming the class has already done the community of learners lesson plan, the teacher can refer to it, reminding students that the class

decided they wanted a classroom of respect and not rudeness. This is just one more reason to honor that commitment.

7. The teacher then writes these two tasks on the board or overhead:

   o What is the most important thing you learned from this lesson? Write a paragraph using the ABC or PQC outline (described in other chapters).

   o The next time you feel like being rude to someone, how can you stop yourself? Fill in the blank in this sentence: "The next time I feel that I'm going to be rude to someone, I will _____ instead."

   Ask students to share what they wrote with a partner and then choose some to share with the class. Make a list of alternative behaviors (walk away, think of something nice, remember how you feel when people are rude to you, etc.) on easel paper to post on a wall.

Assessment

- The ABC/PQC paragraph can serve as an easily assessable product.

- If the teacher feels a more involved assessment is necessary, he or she can develop a simple rubric appropriate for the classroom situation. Free online resources to both find existing rubrics and to create new ones can be found at "The Best Rubric Sites (And A Beginning Discussion About Their Use)" (www.larryferlazzo.edublogs.org/2010/09/18/the-best-rubric-sites-and-a-beginning-discussion-about-their-use).

Possible Extensions

- The teacher could have students read an excerpt from one of the sources listed on the read-aloud.

- Students could be given a piece of paper and colored markers and asked to make a poster. They could label one side "The Next Time I Feel Like Doing This …" and draw themselves being rude (caution students to keep it clean). They could label the other side "I'll Do This, Instead" and draw themselves doing something to avoid the situation (walking away, going back to work, etc.).

- Students could teach what they have learned to another class.

- The teacher could expand the lesson to consider what the best responses might be when a person is being rude to you.

Ed Tech
Making Commercials

Students could use an online application to create a public service announcement encouraging people not to be rude. Sites like Animoto (www.animoto.com) let you manipulate already existing video content to make a short video. You can learn about many similar sites at "The Best Ways For Students To Create Online Videos (Using Someone Else's Content)" (www.larryferlazzo.edublogs.org/2008/05/14/the-best-ways-for-students-to-create-online-videos-using-someone-else%E2%80%99s-content/). This could be combined with a lesson on advertising techniques, like the one on ReadWriteThink called "Persuasive Techniques In Advertising" (http://www.readwritethink.org/classroom-resources/lesson-plans/persuasive-techniques-advertising-1166.html).

Figure 3.2 Rudeness Read-Aloud

What Do Scientific Studies Say About Rudeness?

Being rude, being the target of rudeness, and even witnessing rudeness all have several negative consequences, including:

For the people being rude:

- They suffer a lack of concentration.
- They lose popularity, and their peers and friends become less supportive of them.
- Their peers work to undermine them. (In other words, they try to make the people being rude look bad and not be successful.)

For the people being targeted:

- They become less creative.
- They can't remember as much.
- They don't work as well with others.
- They don't solve problems as well.
- They are more likely to make mistakes.

For the people witnessing rudeness:

- They are more likely to make mistakes.
- They are more likely to think angry thoughts.
- They don't solve problems as well.
- They don't work as well with others.
- They can't remember as much.

Sources: Flin (2010, May 10), Flin (personal communication, July 9, 2010), Jacobson (2008, August 19), Jarrett (2009, May 5), Keen (2009, July 29), Kirby (2010, July 7), Pearson (2010, May 15), Pearson (personal communication, July 9, 2010), Rudeness at Work (2010, July 7), & Spears (2009, August 20).

"Are You a Good Listener or a Bad Listener?" Lesson Plan

Instructional Objectives for Students:

- Identify the characteristics of a good listener and a bad listener.

- Identify the benefits of being a good listener.

- Learn that good listening is an active intellectual process, not just passive.

Duration: Forty minutes

Materials:

- Student copies of Figure 3.3, page 65

- Student copies of Figure 3.4, page 65

- Document camera/overhead projector or easel paper to make chart

Common Core English Language Arts Standards

Writing:

- Produce clear and coherent writing in which the development, organization, and style are appropriate to task, purpose, and audience.

- Use technology, including the Internet, to produce and publish writing and to interact and collaborate with others.

Speaking and Listening:

- Prepare for and participate effectively in a range of conversations and collaborations with diverse partners, building on others' ideas and expressing their own clearly and persuasively.

- Adapt speech to a variety of contexts and communicative tasks, demonstrating command of formal English when indicated or appropriate.

Language:

- Demonstrate command of the conventions of standard English grammar and usage when writing or speaking.

- Demonstrate command of the conventions of standard English capitalization, punctuation, and spelling when writing.

Procedure

1. The teacher explains that the class is going to be talking about listening today. The teacher says he or she is going to distribute a sheet with several quotes (Figure 3.3). Students are to pick one they like, write in their own words what it means, and write why they like it. Students are given a few minutes, then asked to share with a partner. The teacher calls on some to share with the class.

2. The teacher then asks students to think of three or four things they really like and know a lot about—video games, basketball, their family, a favorite book or movie—anything. Students are to list them and take five minutes to write down—not in complete sentences, just notes to remind them—everything they can think of about their topics. The teacher explains that they are going to tell someone else about them.

3. After five minutes, the teacher explains that students will be divided into pairs. One student will speak about his or her topics, and the other will show as many examples of being a bad listener as he or she can think of.

4. After two or three minutes, the teacher asks students to stop. He or she shows a chart, either on the overhead or on easel paper. It is divided into two columns—"Good Listener" on one side and "Bad Listener" on the other. The teacher asks students to share examples of being a bad listener and writes them down. Then the teacher asks the speakers to take a few seconds to think about how they felt when their partners weren't being good listeners, and then asks some of them to share.

5. The teacher explains that now the person who was the bad listener gets to speak, and the other person has to show what it means to be a good listener. Students role-play again for two minutes, and the teacher does a similar listing and discussion process for being a good listener.

6. The teacher explains to students that researchers have found that good listeners feel better about themselves and are more open to new experiences than bad listeners (Engraffia, Graff, Jesuit, & Schall, 1999, p. 23).

7. The teacher explains that he or she is going to put a read-aloud (Figure 3.4) on the overhead that he or she will read. Students should read along silently, and then write in their own words how they could add the ideas in it to the chart under "Good Listener." The teacher reads the read-aloud and gives students a minute or two to write a summary. Students share with a partner, and then the teacher calls on some to share with the class and adds to the chart. The teacher explains that being an active listener is like being an active reader—listeners need to visualize, make connections, ask

questions, summarize, and evaluate—mostly silently in their own minds. The teacher could refer back to the Cuban proverb from the quotations sheet: "Listening looks easy, but it is not simple. Every head is a world."

8. The teacher asks students to copy the chart down.

Assessment

The teacher will ask students to put away their charts and write as many qualities of a good listener as they can remember. The teacher collects students' lists.

Possible Extensions

- Students could make posters illustrating some of the characteristics, possibly picking one bad and one good quality, dividing the paper in two, and labeling one side "If I Feel Like Doing This … " and the other side "Instead, I'll Do This."

- The teacher could ask students to use the ABC or PQC process to write a paragraph about what they have learned.

- The teacher could put Figure 3.5, page 66, on the overhead, read it, and ask students to use the ABC format to answer this question: Why do you think a big business like General Electric would be so concerned about its leaders being good listeners?

Ed Tech
Podcasting

Students could interview one another about what they have learned about the importance of being a good listener and create a short podcast for distribution on the Web. Sites like PodOmatic (www.podomatic.com/) are easy sites to use for recording. For additional options, see "The Best Sites To Practice Speaking English" (www.larryferlazzo. edublogs.org/2008/03/17/the-best-sites-to-practice-speaking-english).

Figure 3.3   Listening Quotations

"If speaking is silver, then listening is gold." —Turkish proverb

"Listening looks easy, but it's not simple. Every head is a world." —Cuban proverb

"Most of the successful people I've known are the ones who do more listening than talking." —attributed to Bernard Baruch, economist and US presidential adviser

"To listen well is as powerful a means of communication and influence as to talk well." —attributed to John Marshall, chief justice of United States

"When one shuts one eye, one does not hear everything." —Swiss proverb

"Nature has give us two ears, two eyes, and but one tongue—to the end that we should hear and see more than we speak." —attributed to Socrates, ancient Greek philosopher

Source: Beck (2010, November 23)

Figure 3.4   Listening Read-Aloud

Good listeners are makers of ideas. Listening involves the reception and processing of incoming data. To listen is not just to hear; it is the active construction of meaning from all the signals—verbal and nonverbal—a speaker is sending. (Hennings, 1992, p. 3)

Second, good listeners are active. They get involved with what they hear, both intellectually and emotionally (Jacobs, 1990). Such listeners give complete attention to what they hear, actively process the information, make pertinent comments and ask relevant questions (Brent & Anderson, 1993).

Source: Excerpt from *Promoting Active Listening in the Classroom,* by Mary Renck Jalongo (1995)

Figure 3.5 Leadership and Listening Read-Aloud

For leaders, listening is a central competence for success. At its core, listening is connecting. Your ability to understand the true spirit of a message as it is intended to be communicated, and to demonstrate your understanding, is paramount in forming connections and leading effectively. This is why, in 2010, General Electric—long considered a preeminent company for producing leaders—redefined what it seeks in its leaders. Now it places listening among the most desirable traits in potential leaders. Indeed, GE chairperson and CEO Jeff Immelt has said that "humble listening" is among the top four characteristics in leaders.

Source: Excerpt from Charan (2012, June 21)

In a study from the ... *Journal of Research in Personality,* former work colleagues rated participants on measures of influence, verbal expression and listening behavior. Results indicate that good listening skills had a stronger effect on the ratings of influence than talking did. The authors suggest that listening helps people obtain information and build trust, both of which can increase influence.

Source: Excerpt from Rodriguez (2012, Dec. 5)

Chapter 4

How Can You Best

Handle Classroom Management?

I know my content and like my students, but sometimes it's hard to get them under control so I can teach my lesson. What tips for classroom management can you give me?

You can never have too many *positive*, not *punitive*, classroom management strategies in your toolbox.

Obviously, there are serious student transgressions, including violence, where some kind of punishment is an appropriate response. However, in many other instances, punishment may work only temporarily, may not work at all, or may only make the problem worse. Research suggests that punishment often primarily teaches the student that he or she just has to be more careful next time to avoid getting caught (Lewis, Romi, Qui, & Katz, 2005).

All the strategies suggested in this chapter—and, in fact, in this book— are grounded in the assumption that teachers recognize that it's absolutely necessary to develop positive, supportive, and public relationships with their students. (More on the idea of "public" will be found later in this chapter.) In addition, this chapter includes many different ideas, because some will work for Bob and not Karen, and others will work for Karen but not for Bob.

The outline for this chapter will follow the model of Chapter 1—first there will be updates on suggestions from *Helping Students Motivate Themselves,* followed by new ideas for immediate actions teachers can take, including a mini-lesson, and then a new lesson plan. Most strategies are designed to help students develop their intrinsic motivation for increasing self-control, though some are more tactical ideas that teachers can use to ensure the classroom runs a little more smoothly.

Updates on "Old" Strategies

Positive Framing

Many studies have reinforced the idea that "loss-framed" messages (if you do this, then something bad will happen to you) really don't have the persuasive advantage that they are thought to have. A recent meta-analysis of multiple studies has found that positive-framed messages (if you do this, all this good stuff will happen to you, like achieving your goals) are more effective (Barker, 2011).

First try talking with your students about how changing their behavior will help them achieve their goals (passing a class, graduating from high school) before threatening negative consequences.

These positive-framed messages pointing out broader student-identified hopes and how they could be connected to students' immediate actions are different from "if /then" incentives that treat them like rats in a maze. Those kinds of extrinsic manipulations are usually focused on what teachers want students to do ("I'll give you extra credit if you don't get out of your seat without permission today"), not on students' self-interest. And, as the first chapter discussed, those kinds of manipulations do not develop higher-order thinking skills or long-term commitments to change.

"Don't Eat the Marshmallow" Lesson

The "Self-Control Lesson Plan" in *Helping Students Motivate Themselves* (Ferlazzo, 2011, p. 57) taught students about Dr. Walter Mischel's famous marshmallow experiment. Small children were placed in a room alone, and a marshmallow was put in front of each child. An adult told the child that he or she would stay in the room with the marshmallow for fifteen minutes. If the child refrained from eating it during that time, he or she would get a second marshmallow. Children who demonstrated self-control during the fifteen minutes—many used the strategy of distracting themselves from the marshmallow—were found to be far more successful years in the future. In the lesson plan, students read about the study, watched a video of a replicated experiment (de Posada, 2009), identified times they did not exhibit self-control, and developed specific plans to distract themselves when they felt those temptations in the future ("If I am tempted to throw a spitball at John, then I will instead remember the time John helped me with my homework").

In 2010, the results of two similar rigorous experiments that spanned decades were released. These studies, following hundreds of young people through adulthood in New Zealand and in Great Britain, reached similar conclusions to those of Mischel's study—those who demonstrated greater self-control in primary school had fewer health problems, higher academic achievement, greater financial success, and increased family stability as adults (Moffitt et al., 2011).

Another study released in 2012 found that young children who were able to pay attention and persist with a task had a 50 percent greater chance of completing college. Its research concluded that assessments of self-control were a better predictor of college success than early math and reading skills (Oregon State University, 2012).

In addition to sharing with students these new studies that reaffirm the marshmallow experiment's findings, we can make students aware of the conclusions of Nobel Prize winner James Heckman (mentioned in the Introduction). He has found that there are two key points in a young person's life when he or she is most likely to be successful in developing long-term character traits like self-control and perseverance—early childhood and adolescence (Ferlazzo, 2012, July 8). As they learn about the ramifications of the Marshmallow Experiment, students need to know that their lives have not been predetermined by how they have acted in the past or how they are acting now. What matters most is how they will act in the future. As Mischel said, "It is not simply that life does things to us. But we in turn do things to it .... This reflects dynamic interaction through which people change" ("Walter Mischel's," 2011).

An excellent video to incorporate into the "Self-Control Lesson Plan," or to even use on its own, is an eight-minute segment from *PBS NewsHour*. It's called "'Sesame Street' Tells You How to Get to Sunnier Days Financially," and in it economics correspondent Paul Solman has an informative and engaging conversation about both Mischel's study and the New Zealand/Great Britain study with Elmo from *Sesame Street*. Students of all ages would enjoy this segment; the video and a transcript are available online for free ("'Sesame Street,'" 2011).

Recent studies have also reinforced the importance of preparing the kind of "if/then" replacement strategies ("If I am tempted to yell at my sister, then I will instead look away and count to ten") suggested in the lesson plan (Hoffman & Friese, 2011; "Seven ways to be good," n.d.). Of course, it's important that these targeted temptations be identified by the student, not the teacher (though the teacher can raise questions and offer ideas). In fact, Mischel recently pointed out that self-control is not just a matter of gritting our teeth and toughing things out. He calls it "a strategic allocation of attention" that requires developing ways to distract ourselves from the temptation, and an "if/then" plan fits the bill (Lehrer, 2012b). Another recent study attempted a version of the marshmallow test using texting. Subjects received texts while they were watching a video lecture, and those who waited the longest to respond, or did not respond at all, did best on a subsequent test they took on the information given in the lecture (Sparks, 2012). It's likely that most teachers would love their students to develop an "if/then" implementation plan related to texts! (It's important to note that these kind of "if/then" plans are different from the "if/then" rewards strategy criticized earlier—if you do this, then I'll give you this).

Ian Ayres (2011), a professor of law and economics at Yale, revisited the data in Mischel's study and shared his own analysis in *The New York Times*. He suggests that the results show a more nuanced conclusion than is generally written about publicly. He concludes the findings were not "all or nothing"—the study did not show that if a child didn't resist the marshmallow for fifteen minutes, then he or she would likely do very badly in life. Ayres writes that it was instead a matter of gradation—children who waited fifteen minutes scored about 210 points higher on their SATs than those who couldn't wait at all, but those who waited five minutes scored about 100 points higher. Making that point clear to our students could be very valuable—it's not a question of having to show complete self-control all of the time. It's more a matter of showing self-control more often than not.

A new study offers another possible addition to the "Self-Control Lesson Plan." Using a piece of chocolate cake instead of a marshmallow, researchers determined that having people think about the pride that they will feel in themselves after resisting temptation was a very successful self-control strategy. And, interestingly enough, trying to encourage self-control through the use of shame or guilt actually resulted in people showing *less* self-control (MacInnis, 2011). When students identify the temptations they want to resist near the end of the lesson, and the strategies they are going to use to resist them, it would be easy to add a third part: "Write how you will feel when you demonstrate self-control successfully." This strategy of emphasizing pride over shame and guilt could also offer a general guideline to teachers when handling any behavioral issues.

Finally, one last addition to this lesson plan, and multiple others, could be a self-persuasion essay that recent studies have found helpful ("How to Encourage People," 2012; Markman, 2012a). One effective way to convince yourself of something is to imagine that you have to convince someone else, whether you agree with the position or not. Writing a persuasive essay using this frame (making a case for the importance of self-control) could not only be a good review of the information covered in a lesson, but could also solidify student commitments to implementing changes (not to mention providing a opportunity for writing practice!).

Replenishing Self-Control

Countless studies have found that self-control is a resource that can get depleted after heavy use, and that it can be replenished in several different ways ("Self-Control Instantly Replenished," 2010). One strategy building on that research is the use of "reflection cards" that are given immediately after disruptive behavior or, ideally, are taken by students when they feel they are near that point. Students would respond to two requests on the cards:

1. Please write at least three sentences about a time (or times) you have felt successful and happy.
2. Please write at least three sentences about something that is important to you (friends, family, sports, etc.) and why it's important.

In many cases, that simple act appears to replenish student self-control.

Recent studies have confirmed the finding that self-control is a finite resource. Here's how one new study described it: "Once the pool has dried up, we're less likely to keep our cool the next time we're faced with a situation that requires self-control" ("This Is Your Brain," 2012).

This study, though, did more than just develop a new analogy to describe self-control. For the first time, researchers were able to take brain scans when a person was showing self-control and when the person had run out of patience. Those images are freely available online, included at the same link cited for the pool analogy.

Showing students these images might be a good reminder that they can indeed control much of what physically occurs inside their brains.

"New" Strategies for Immediate Responses

Here are several classroom management strategies that teachers can keep in mind during day-to-day work in school.

Goal Reminders

The same study mentioned earlier that took scans of a brain when it was demonstrating self-control and when it was showing impatience also came to another intriguing conclusion. Researchers found that reminding people about the negative consequences of losing self-control was not effective at getting them to regain it. The intervention that did work, though, was asking them to take a minute to think about behaviors they needed to exhibit to achieve their goals.

Of course, for a teacher to implement this strategy successfully, he or she needs to have a positive relationship with students, in order to know their goals.

Before, during, or after implementing this intervention and others discussed in this book, the research behind them can be shared with students so that they can work toward self-intervention when they are facing challenges. We teachers will obviously not be with them most of the time, so the more tools students can have in their own toolbox, the greater sense of self-efficacy they will feel (which in turn generates more motivation).

Postpone

One recent study found that making a conscious decision to postpone giving in to temptation (in the study's case, eating potato chips) can be an effective strategy in reducing a desire (Society for Personality and Social Psychology, 2012). How could this idea be applied in the classroom? One of my students had been constantly using her phone to text during class. I didn't want to take her phone away, so instead I made a deal with her—she could use it openly in my classroom as soon as she entered the room until the bell rang, and she could use it openly when the lunch bell rang until she left (I would be closing my eyes to a school rule against using cell phones at all during the school day). Since we made that deal, she hardly ever used her cell phone during class. But, even more significantly, she hardly ever used her cell phone during the times we agreed she could, either.

Use Non-Active Words

Another study found that using non-active words like *stop* and *pause* might help people resist temptation more than active words like *fight* or *control*. If, in some cases, students are having difficulties following the distraction strategies they've developed as part of the "Self-Control Lesson" in *Helping Students Motivate Themselves*, or if that lesson plan has not yet been taught, a teacher could use this knowledge in a "sticky note" strategy. For example, I have had students place sticky notes on their desks at the beginning of class where they have written non-active words of their choice that serve as ongoing reminders of the behaviors they want to resist.

This, of course, takes place only after I have a conversation with the students where I share the research and we agree to try it out for a period of time to see if it works. It has had a positive effect more often than not.

Public Versus Private Relationships

Community organizers try to help people understand the difference between public and private relationships. Often, those in power will try to blur that division when it suits their purposes (for example, politicians kissing babies). Here is another example: I have spent time over the years working with many organizations, including religious congregations, to make community improvements. The political decision makers with whom we would have to negotiate were sometimes members of those congregations, and they would often try to persuade pastors or congregation leaders to take a different public position. The religious leaders, in turn, would point out that public relationships and public dialogue should be had *publicly*, whereas private relationships and private dialogues should be had *privately*. In public life, relationships are conditional—based on negotiation and reciprocity. In private life, relationships are often based on love and friendship. This distinction was particularly important to demonstrate in public settings.

And we carried this distinction over to how members needed to act in the context of the organization—at our meetings, with the media, and whenever they were in the public eye.

I apply this concept in the classroom by helping students understand the difference between public behavior and private behavior. When students are in the classroom, it is a public space with certain expectations. One small example is a student shouting out "I'm bored" or some other inappropriate comment.

One possible response to that kind of remark is a sharp admonishment from the teacher. Instead, though, what I generally do is—either right then or at the next available opportunity—go over the student, put my arm around his or her shoulders, and have this kind of quick dialogue, with a smile:

Me: Johnny, is it okay for you to think what you said?

Johnny: Yes.

Me: Johnny, is it okay for you to tell your friends after class what you just said?

Johnny: Yes.

Me: Johnny, is it okay for you to say what you just said out loud in the classroom?

Johnny: No.

And with both of us smiling, it's over.

I sometimes will have done it enough times with a student that when I go over, he or she will recite all of the lines. Notice that the dialogue leads with what students *can* do, instead of what they *can't*.

These kinds of inappropriate comments seem to decrease as the school year goes on as at least some students gain a greater understanding of the differences between public and private, an understanding that should serve them well for years to come.

The Benjamin Franklin Effect

The Benjamin Franklin effect is named after a strategy Franklin used to gain political support from rivals—he asked them for a favor. He found that "you grow to like people for whom you do nice things and hate people you harm" ("The Benjamin Franklin Effect," 2011).

Many teachers know that giving unpredictable students positions of classroom responsibility can often result in a major behavioral change for the better.

Being Authoritative, Not Authoritarian

Being authoritarian typically means using power unilaterally for control without any explanation given and with obedience demanded. Being authoritative, on the other hand, means demonstrating strong control, but doing so relationally by listening and explaining. Studies of parenting styles have found that parents using an authoritative style were viewed by children as legitimate authority figures and, as a result, were less likely to engage in delinquent behavior. The opposite was true for authoritarian parents (University of New Hampshire, 2012).

It's not too much of a stretch to apply the same findings to our classrooms and, in fact, classroom studies on self-control, also known as self-regulation, have come to similar conclusions (Willingham, 2011, p. 25). Which of the two styles do we want to emulate? Do we always lead with our mouths, or do we just as often lead with our ears? Do we believe that we are always the "sage on stage"? Do we think it's important to have students periodically complete class and teacher evaluations and seriously consider what they write, or do we believe what they think is of little or no consequence? Do we think it's important to explain why we teach lessons the way we do, and be open to hearing from students that there might be better ways to do it?

Doodling

Most teachers prefer student eye contact when they are speaking, or having students' eyes on something being displayed as teachers talk about it. We can ask for it, and push for it, but it's just a losing battle with some students.

When that happens, we can turn a problem into an opportunity.

A recent study shows that people doodling had a much higher recall of information they were listening to than those who were not doodling, perhaps because "doodling aids cognitive performance by reducing day-dreaming" (Barker, 2010).

Instead of a having a battle with those students who, for whatever reason, find it challenging to constantly look up, teachers could make a deal with them (as I have on occasion). There will be times when the teacher makes a point of asking *all* students to look at something on the overhead, but at other times, those students can doodle.

Cues and Habit Formation

Research has found a universal three-step process for habit formation—a cue (a trigger for some kind of automatic behavior), a routine, and a reward (Ferlazzo, 2012, June 5). One of the easiest ways a teacher can intervene in a student's disruptive habit is by removing the cue (Willingham, 2011, p. 26)—moving a student's seat (or that of a neighboring classmate), for example. Of course, changing a student's seat to alter a behavior is an age-old classroom management strategy. However, discussing the idea of habit formation and eliciting from students what cues might provoke their behavior is an activity that many of us overlook.

"What Would Be the Long-Term Effect of Doing That?"

Educator and positive classroom management consultant Marvin Marshall recommends a simple strategy of—either in the moment or afterward—asking a disruptive student a simple question: "What would be the long-term effect of doing that?" (Marshall, 2011). As he suggests, asking can be far more effective than telling.

Alternatives to Collective Punishment

I suspect many teachers have had an experience like this:

A paper airplane, ball of paper, or pencil flies through the air, or somebody makes an obnoxious noise. The object is probably aimed at another student, and it may or may not hit the intended target. The noise is just meant to be funny.

You can tell the general area it came from, but you don't really know who the culprit is. It's frustrating because that kind of behavior does not contribute to a learning community.

What do you do?

It's not uncommon for teachers to first yell something like, "Who threw it?" No one admits to it, and then the teacher will punish the entire group.

Here's a definition of collective punishment:

> Collective punishment is the punishment of a group of people as a result of the behavior of one or more other individuals or groups. The punished group may often have no direct association with the other individuals or groups, or direct control over their actions. ("Collective Punishment," n.d.)

I'm not convinced that this behavior is one we want to model for our students. If collective punishment is out, then what are the alternatives?

This kind of misbehavior does not happen that often in my classes, thankfully, but it certainly does occur. What I usually do is go over to the area where I suspect the noise or projectile originated and quietly explain that I don't feel respected when this kind of thing happens. And, since I feel like I show that I respect students at all times, I would hope they would want me to feel respected. I then explain that I don't know who actually did it, but that I would like each of them to commit that they will not throw something (or make a noise, etc.), and we shake on it. I tell them that I'm sure they are people of their word, and the matter is closed.

Nine times out of ten, that is the end of things, and there is no repetition. However, if it does happen again, I go to the next step. For example, somebody in my class was occasionally making an obnoxious noise. I knew it was one of two students. I did the first step with them, and that went fine. Then, two days later, one of them made the noise again.

I asked them both to come outside with me, and I explained that I was disappointed that one of them was not keeping their word. I knew that one was trustworthy, but I didn't know which one. So I said that I couldn't trust the word of either of them and didn't like feeling that way. I suggested that the person who was making the noise might want to think about how his or her actions were now affecting the other student. Then, I gave them a few minutes to talk about it privately (I left the door open and asked them to stay in front of it so I could observe their actions, but not overhear what they said).

There wasn't an obnoxious noise again.

So in other words, the second step, when necessary, is to ask students to consider the impact their actions have on others, and ask them to try to work out problems among themselves. In my teaching career, this has almost always resulted in stopping the inappropriate behavior and, I hope, students gaining some added maturity.

Of course, one of the most common situations where the specter of collective punishment is raised is after a difficult time with a substitute teacher. One preventative strategy is the use of Figure 4.1, page 80. Early in the year, the teacher shows the simple rubric to students and explains that a substitute will use it with them. Five minutes prior to the end of class with the sub, he or she will distribute the rubrics, and students will write down their names and grade themselves. The sub will then go around, give what grade he or she believes the student has earned, and collect the sheets (this process means the sub does not have to worry about remembering individual names and can base the evaluation on student faces).

This can be a very effective strategy to reduce teacher temptation to inflict collective punishment on a class, enhance the likelihood of a class with a sub being somewhat productive, and dramatically reduce stress for the sub.

After a class has shown that it understands and respects the expected behavior, a teacher can experiment with not using the grading rubric and explaining to students that he or she trusts that they will act appropriately.

Which leads us to the next strategy …

Reminder of Moral Values

Behavioral economist Dan Ariely (2012) found in one experiment that if people are reminded of their moral values they are far less likely to cheat. In his study, they were reminded of the Ten Commandments.

A variation of this study can be applied if a teacher knows that a substitute will be coming the next day. In less than a minute, a teacher can remind students of the expected behavior, say that he or she would like to be able to trust them, and ask students to raise their hands if they commit to the expected behavior. Similar exercises could be used before going to a school assembly or a computer lab.

In my experience, I have always found a clear difference in student behavior between when I do this kind of reminder and when I do not.

The Zeigarnik Effect

The Zeigarnik effect, which builds on our natural need for closure (Konnikova, 2012c), was discussed in Chapter 1. When students do not want to work, we can ask them to get started by just writing a first line or answering the easiest question. This can prompt them to want to continue on their own.

Light Touches

Studies have shown that a supportive touch on the shoulder can result in a student being twice as likely to volunteer in class than if he or she did not receive that touch. When checking out books at a library, those who were touched on the hand or arm by the employee behind the desk rated the library more favorably afterwards. People dining at restaurants who are casually touched by waiters or waitresses feel more positively about their experience and leave higher tips ("Why Is a Touch," 2011). Numerous other studies suggest that touch can have additional positive cognitive effects (Carey, 2010).

Of course, teachers have to be careful using this tactic, but a quick shoulder touch should be doable for many.

Positive Bias

When a teacher talks to a student privately about his or her behavior in the classroom, sometimes the student might claim he or she did nothing wrong (Teacher: "How do you think you handled yourself in class?" Student: "I did fine." Teacher: "I didn't feel respected by you in class when you _____." Student: "Don't make a big deal out of nothing."). In these situations, the student is probably "positive biased" in self-reporting his or her behavior (Gosling, John, Craik, & Robins, 1998, p. 1345). In other words, he or she is likely to have an unrealistically favorable impression of his or her own performance.

This same positive bias can arise in other situations. For example, after a student who has been facing behavioral challenge has a good day, the teacher might ask how the student is feeling and help him or her contrast that with how he or she has felt after more difficult days. More often than not, this leads to a fruitful conversation about what the student did differently. But not always. Some students don't see, or are unable to acknowledge, the difference in their behavior.

Here's a mini-lesson on this topic that, after it is done in class, can be referred to when students are showing positive bias during discussions with them about classroom behavior.

Mini-Lesson: Positive Bias

1. The teacher places Figure 4.2, page 81, on the overhead and asks students to read along silently as he or she reads it to the class. The teacher covers up everything other than the Benjamin Franklin quote and asks students to take two minutes to write a response to

a question he or writes on the whiteboard or below the read-aloud: "What do you think Franklin meant, and do you agree with him? Why or why not?"

2. The teacher asks students to quickly do a pair-share and asks some to share what they wrote with the class.

3. The teacher then uncovers the rest of the read-aloud and reads it to the class. He or she explains that some researchers call this positive bias and writes the phrase on the board or overhead. The teacher explains that we all tend to have a higher opinion of our behavior than is true. He or she then gives two examples, one professional and one personal (for example, what he or she learned from how students have evaluated classes, or about a time when he or she thought she was fine at home but a spouse said accurately that he or she had been grumpy). She also distributes copies of the read-aloud to all students.

4. The teacher asks students to think of two instances—one at school and one at home—when, in retrospect, they think they might have been positively biased in seeing how they were acting (in a class, with friends, with a boyfriend or girlfriend, with a parent, etc.). The teacher asks them to write down their ideas, share with a different partner, and then has a few students share with the class.

5. The teacher can say that the point of this short lesson is not that we are *always* wrong about how we judge ourselves, and or that everyone else is *always* right in their judgments of us. Instead, it's important to remember that we *often* are not the best judges of our behavior, and that we can *often* learn a great deal by taking seriously the opinions others have about our actions.

6. The teacher then asks students to write a paragraph using the ABC format (Answer the question; Back it up with a quote or other evidence; make a Connection to an experience or another text) that answers this question: "What is positive bias?" Students can then share verbally with a partner and give their papers to the teacher.

Setting the Stage

Student Stress

This section contains an engaging lesson plan designed to help students develop their intrinsic motivation toward increasing self-control. Stress, especially among teens, has been shown to reduce a person's self-control

Figure 4.1 Behavior and Attitude with Substitute Teacher

Student name _____

Category	A	B	C	D
Focus on the learning task	Consistently stayed focused on the learning task and what needed to be done. Very self-directed.	Focused on the learning task and what needed to be done most of the time.	Focused on the learning task and what needed to be done some of the time. The substitute teacher had to remind him or her often to stay focused on the task.	Rarely focused on the learning task and did not complete it.
Attitude and behavior	Never had to be reminded to be well-behaved and helpful to the substitute teacher.	Had to be reminded once to be well-behaved and helpful to the substitute teacher.	Had to be reminded twice to be well-behaved and helpful to the substitute teacher.	Had to be reminded more than twice to be well-behaved and helpful to the substitute teacher.

Student comments and grade:

Substitute teacher comments and grade:

Student: You must complete this rubric and give it to the substitute when he or she requests it. This activity is worth one hundred points. I cannot believe I will have to do this with anyone, but you will receive an automatic F on this rubric if you do not turn it in and you do not have an excused absence.

Figure 4.2   Evaluating Ourselves Read-Aloud

"There are three things extremely hard: steel, a diamond, and to know one's self."

—Benjamin Franklin, *Poor Richard's Improved Almanack* (1750)

"Around one million students were asked how good they were at getting along with others, 85% rated themselves above the median and 25% rated themselves in the top 1%.... Far more than 50% of people rank themselves in the top half of driving ability.... And most men rank themselves in the top half of male athletic ability."

Source: Keller (2012, June 14)

capacity (Begley & Chatzky, 2011). A teacher's ability to control the amount of stress in a student's life is limited, but the "Stress Lesson Plan" in this chapter is designed to help students learn the negative impact stress can have on their minds and their health, and to expose them to strategies they can use to reduce its effect on them. One other action a teacher can take is to try to reduce stress in their classroom for students. Studies have shown that the more powerless you feel in a situation, the greater stress you feel (Lehrer, 2012a). Implementing many of the strategies suggested in this book can result in students feeling that they are more "learning with" instead of being "taught to," and this feeling—and reality—can help reduce stress.

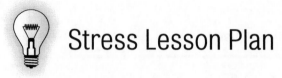# Stress Lesson Plan

Instructional Objectives for Students:

- Use inductive learning to gain a better understanding of stress, its dangers, and what can be done to combat it.

- Read complex texts related to stress.

- Write a very simple essay about stress and learn a technique on how to organize and write future essays.

- Develop strategies on how they will combat stress in their own lives.

Duration: Four sixty-minute periods, but that can be reduced to three if the visit to the computer lab is eliminated

Materials:

- An overhead projector or document camera, a computer projector, and Internet access

- Paper for individual student posters and colored pencils or markers

- Student copies of Figure 4.3, page 88, and Figure 4.4, page 91

- Highlighters, glue sticks, and scissors for all students

- Student copies of "Helping Teenagers With Stress" by the American Academy of Child & Adolescent Psychiatry (downloadable at www.aacap.org/cs/root/facts_for_families/helping_teenagers_with_stress)

- Student access to a computer lab or laptop cart

- 11" x 14" sheets of paper for all students

Common Core English Language Arts Standards

Reading: Determine central ideas or themes of a text and analyze their development; summarize the key supporting details and ideas.

Writing: Produce clear and coherent writing in which the development, organization, and style are appropriate to task, purpose, and audience.

Speaking and Listening: Prepare for and participate effectively in a range of conversations and collaborations with diverse partners, building on others' ideas and expressing their own clearly and persuasively.

Language: Demonstrate command of the conventions of standard English grammar and usage when writing or speaking.

Procedure

First Day:

1. Students enter the room with this question and instructions written on the board or on the overhead: "Please answer in writing: When was the last time you felt stressed and why? (If you don't feel comfortable sharing the last time, pick another time.) You have three minutes."

2. After three minutes, the teacher says he or she will explain why the class is doing this in a few minutes, but right now he or she wants students to verbally share what they wrote with a partner and then asks a few students to share what they wrote with the class.

3. The teacher announces that stress is an important issue in all our lives, and that the class will learn about it over the next few days.

4. The teacher passes out Figure 4.3. He or she explains that students will break into pairs and take turns reading each passage aloud to their partners. While they are reading each passage, students are to highlight three to five words that communicate the most important information. In addition, after reading each passage students need to demonstrate a reading strategy—they write a question about the passage, visualize by drawing a picture (and write a sentence saying what the picture is), make a connection to themselves or another text, evaluate it by agreeing or disagreeing and explaining why, or summarize it in one sentence. Students need to use at least three different reading strategies and have to annotate each passage (so a strategy will be used more than once). The teacher models doing it on the first passage. He or she tells students to ignore the list of categories at the top for now. Students will have twenty minutes to complete the data set.

5. Students are given highlighters, pair up, and begin reading.

6. The teacher brings students back together as a class and calls on one person for each of the eight passages to quickly share either the words they highlighted or the reading strategy they used. This should not take more than five or six minutes.

7. The teacher now draws the class's attention to the list of three categories at the top of Figure 4.3. He or she explains that students are going to return to their partners and identify which category each of the passages belong in. Students can write the words Brain, Body, or Handle (to represent each of the categories) next to a passage and circle the word or phrase that provides evidence for it belonging in that category. The teacher models doing

that for the first passage by writing Handle next to it and circling the phrase "work on developing these attitudes and behaviors." He or she explains that students will have ten minutes to complete the categorizing activity.

8. Students return to their partners and do the categorization.

9. Ten minutes later the teacher brings the class back together. He or she calls out the number for each passage and asks a student to say the category and provide the evidence (the circled words). The teacher can ask people to raise their hands if they agree. If some disagree, the teacher can ask what they think. As long as people can provide reasonable evidence to support their positions, their answers are correct.

10. The teacher either asks students to write their names on their Figure 4.3 sheets and hand them in or has them hold on to them until tomorrow.

Second Day:

1. The teacher explains that they are going to continue with their lesson on stress. He or she distributes 11" x 14" sheets of paper, scissors, and glue, and tells students that they are to write the names of each category at the top of a column, then cut out and paste each appropriate passage underneath it. They must leave space in each column for additional information. Students are given fifteen minutes to complete this activity.

2. The teacher tells students that they are going to watch a very short PBS report on what stress does to the teenage brain. They are to watch it and write down new information in the appropriate category. The teacher shows the video, located at www.nsf.gov/news/special_reports/science_nation/teensstress.jsp.

3. After the video, the teacher calls on a few students to share what they wrote with the class.

4. The teacher then distributes copies of the "Helping Teenagers With Stress" handout, and tells students to work with a partner different from the one they had yesterday to identify a few new pieces of information they can add to the appropriate category. Students are given seven minutes.

5. The teacher gives a preview of the next day by explaining that they will be going to the computer lab (or perhaps they can all be given laptops from a cart). They will have thirty minutes to find more information online that fits into each category. Then, they can take some online tests to evaluate their own stress levels at "The Best Resources For Learning About Teens & Stress" (www.larryferlazzo.edublogs.org/2011/06/19/the-best-resources-for-learning-about-teens-stress). There are also links at that address they can use for researching more information. On a separate piece of paper they can write notes about what they learn from the online stress tests.

6. The teacher then explains that one way we can reduce our stress is by being conscious of how we breathe. He or she goes to www.kidshealth.org/teen/your_mind/emotions/stress.html?tracking=81452_A# and the class practices the breathing exercise that is demonstrated.

7. The teacher collects the categorized posters.

Third Day:

1. The teacher returns the posters, repeats the instructions from the day before, and takes the class to the computer lab. After thirty minutes, he or she tells students to start taking the stress tests and take notes on what they learn.

2. After twenty minutes of exploring the stress tests, they can pair up and share what they learned by taking the tests—but only information they feel comfortable sharing.

3. The teacher collects the categorization sheet with new information, but students can keep their notes on the stress tests.

Fourth Day:

1. . The teacher explains that students are going to complete the unit on stress today.

2. The teacher places Figure 4.4 on the overhead and explains that this is an easy way to organize their notes. He or she says students will receive a copy of it, and they are to look in their categories of information and write no more than two words on each line coming from the category circles in the organizer. The teachers shows the examples that are already there and says that students will have no more than fifteen minutes to complete it.

3. Students work individually on their graphic organizers with the teacher circulating throughout the room.

4. At the end of fifteen minutes, the teacher asks students to stop and put their category posters away. Students should just have the graphic organizer and a blank sheet of paper on their desks. The teacher explains that for the next fifteen minutes, students will write the middle three paragraphs of a five paragraph essay just using their graphic organizer, without looking at their category poster. This will push students to put their essay completely in their own words. Students should leave space at the top of their paper for the introduction paragraph and space at the bottom for the conclusion. To begin writing, students should first think about what would be a good logical order of paragraphs for the three categories. Second, they should think carefully about writing a topic sentence for each of their three paragraphs, and then use the notes to complete them.

5. At the end of fifteen minutes, whether or not all students are done, the teacher should ask them to stop for a moment and tell them they can continue in a few minutes. The teacher then explains they have to write an introduction, including a hook (a question, an interesting fact or story, a quotation, something humorous, etc.), a thesis statement, and then a sentence describing what will be in the essay. In an ideal world, this will not be the first time students have been exposed to the components of an essay—the point of this lesson is less to teach the qualities of an essay and more to have students learn a new way to prepare for writing one.

6. Students are given five minutes to write an introduction paragraph.

7. Next, the teacher explains the parts of a conclusion—a restatement of the thesis statement and the key points in the essay, and a statement about why the topic is important. Students are given five minutes to write a conclusion.

8. Even if students are not done, the teacher asks them to stop and explains that, in addition to learning about stress, this whole lesson was designed to help students learn a new way to research and write an essay. First, students should organize their research into categories. Next, they should identify only the most important pieces of information in each category. And, lastly, they can turn the categories into paragraphs and the paragraphs into an essay.

9. Students can then turn in their essays if they are completed, or complete them as homework.

10. The teacher explains that in the last ten minutes of class, he or she wants students to think about the techniques they learned to handle stress. He or she wants students to take this time to make a simple poster on a small piece of paper saying this at the top: "When I feel stressed, I will _____" and fill in the blank with one, two, or three actions they will take. Then, below it, they can illustrate the action or actions they chose. The teacher can distribute colored pencils and paper, and students can complete the poster in class or at home. The teacher can collect the posters for display around the classroom.

Assessment

- The essay should be an easily assessable student product.

- If desired, teachers could develop their own rubrics for use with this activity. See "The Best Rubric Sites (And A Beginning Discussion About Their Use)" (www.larryferlazzo.edublogs.org/2010/09/18/the-best-rubric-sites-and-a-beginning-discussion-about-their-use) for multiple free online tools for creating rubrics.

Possible Extensions

- If there is a class blog, students could post their essays there and comment on one another's work.

- Students could create posters offering advice on coping with stress that could be posted around the school.

Ed Tech

Animation

Students could create online animations portraying stressful events and how they might handle them. There are many free and easy applications for creating them, and a list of the best ones can be found at "The Best Ways For Students To Create Online Animations" (www.larryferlazzo.edublogs.org/2008/05/11/the-best-ways-for-students-to-create-online-animations).

Figure 4.3   Stress Data Set

Categories: What stress does to your brain; What stress does to your body; Ways to handle stress

1. Ever notice that certain people seem to adapt quickly to stressful circumstances and take things in stride? They're cool under pressure and able to handle problems as they come up. Researchers have identified the qualities that make some people seem naturally resilient even when faced with high levels of stress.

     If you want to build your resilience, work on developing these attitudes and behaviors:

   ▪ Think of change as a challenging and normal part of life.

   ▪ See setbacks and problems as temporary and solvable.

   ▪ Believe that you will succeed if you keep working toward your goals.

   ▪ Take action to solve problems that crop up.

   ▪ Build strong relationships and keep commitments to family and friends.

   ▪ Have a support system and ask for help.

   ▪ Participate regularly in activities for relaxation and fun.

   (Stress, n.d., © 1995–2012. The Nemours Foundation/KidsHealth®. Reprinted with permission. www.kidshealth.org/teen/your_mind/emotions/stress.html?tracking=81452_A#)

2. The human body responds to stressors by activating the nervous system and specific hormones. The hypothalamus signals the adrenal glands to produce more of the hormones adrenaline and cortisol and release them into the blood-stream. These hormones speed up heart rate, breathing rate, blood pressure, and metabolism. Blood vessels open wider to let more blood flow to large muscle groups, putting our muscles on alert. Pupils dilate to improve vision. The liver releases some of its stored glucose to increase the body's energy. And sweat is produced to cool the body. All of these physical changes prepare a person to react quickly and effectively to handle the pressure of the moment. This natural reaction is known as the stress response. Working properly, the body's stress response enhances a person's ability to perform well under pressure. But the stress response can also cause problems when it overreacts or fails to turn off and reset itself properly. (Stress, n.d., © 1995–2012. The Nemours Foundation/KidsHealth®. Reprinted with permission. www.kidshealth.org/teen/your_mind/emotions/stress.html?tracking=81452_A#)

3. One researcher found that rats subjected to stress for an hour forgot how to move through a maze: "If uncontrollable stress disrupts rats' abilities to adjust their behaviour," she said, "how influenced by stress are people's frequent and complex daily decisions?" "Stress causes neurons (brain cells) to shrink or grow," said Bruce McEwen, a neuroscientist at Rockefeller University in New York. "The wear and tear on the body from lots of stress changes the nervous system" ("Studies show stress", 2008).

(continued)

Figure 4.3 Stress Data Set (*continued*)

4. Chronic stress, the stress we all experience in our everyday life, like trying to get to work or school on time, typically does not make the size of the brain shrink by an amount we should be worried about. However, the problem occurs when we experience a major event that causes a significant amount of stress:

> That's because chronic stress may erode parts of the brain gradually, just enough so it's not perceptible but, enough that when a truly stressful event occurs, its effects are magnified and our ability to cope is compromised "Over time, as the number of cumulative stressors increases, chronic stress can interact with that and worsen the effect," says [Dr. Rajita Sinha]. (Park, 2012)

5. The stress response (also called the fight or flight response) is critical during emergency situations, such as when a driver has to slam on the brakes to avoid an accident. It can also be activated in a milder form at a time when the pressure's on but there's no actual danger—like stepping up to take the foul shot that could win the game, getting ready to go to a big dance, or sitting down for a final exam. A little of this stress can help keep you on your toes, ready to rise to a challenge. And the nervous system quickly returns to its normal state, standing by to respond again when needed. But stress doesn't always happen in response to things that are immediate or that are over quickly. Ongoing or long-term events, like coping with a divorce or moving to a new neighborhood or school, can cause stress, too. Long-term stressful situations can produce a lasting, low-level stress that's hard on people. The nervous system senses continued pressure and may remain slightly activated and continue to pump out extra stress hormones over an extended period. This can wear out the body's reserves, leave a person feeling depleted or overwhelmed, weaken the body's immune system, and cause other problems. (Stress, n.d., © 1995–2012. The Nemours Foundation/KidsHealth®. Reprinted with permission. www.kidshealth.org/teen/your_mind/emotions/stress.html?tracking=81452_A#)

6. When the stressors of your life are always present, leaving you constantly feeling stressed, tense, nervous or on edge, that fight-or-flight reaction stays turned on. The less control you have over potentially stress-inducing events and the more uncertainty they create, the more likely you are to feel stressed. Even the typical day-to-day demands of living can contribute to your body's stress response.

   The long-term activation of the stress-response system—and the subsequent overexposure to cortisol and other stress hormones—can disrupt almost all your body's processes. This puts you at increased risk of numerous health problems, including:

■ Heart disease   ■ Depression

■ Sleep problems   ■ Obesity

■ Digestive problems   ■ Memory impairment

■ Worsening of skin conditions, such as eczema

(Stress: Constant stress, n.d., www.mayoclinic.com/health/stress/SR00001 Mayo Foundation for Medical Education and Research, Reprinted with permission)

(continued)

Figure 4.3   Stress Data Set (*continued*)

7. Experts agree that getting regular exercise helps people manage stress. (Excessive or compulsive exercise can contribute to stress, though, so as in all things, use moderation.) And eat well to help your body get the right fuel to function at its best. It's easy when you're stressed out to eat on the run or eat junk food or fast food. But under stressful conditions, the body needs its vitamins and minerals more than ever. Some people may turn to substance abuse as a way to ease tension. Although alcohol or drugs may seem to lift the stress temporarily, relying on them to cope with stress actually promotes more stress because it wears down the body's ability to bounce back. (Stress, n.d., © 1995–2012. The Nemours Foundation/KidsHealth®. Reprinted with permission. www.kidshealth. org/teen/your_mind/emotions/stress.html?tracking=81452_A#)

8. Research has found that smiling can reduce your stress level. "The results of the study suggest that smiling may actually influence our physical state: compared to participants who held neutral facial expressions, participants who were instructed to smile, and in particular those with Duchenne smiles [genuine smiles with your eyes as well as your mouth], had lower heart rate levels after recovery from the stressful activities. . . .These findings show that smiling during brief stressors can help to reduce the intensity of the body's stress response, regardless of whether a person actually feels happy.

    "The next time you are stuck in traffic or are experiencing some other type of stress," says [Sarah] Pressman, "you might try to hold your face in a smile for a moment. Not only will it help you 'grin and bear it' psychologically, but it might actually help your heart health as well!" (Grin and bear it!, 2012, www. psychologicalscience.org/index.php/news/releases/smiling-facilitates-stress-recovery.html, reprinted with permission)

Figure 4.4 Graphic Organizer

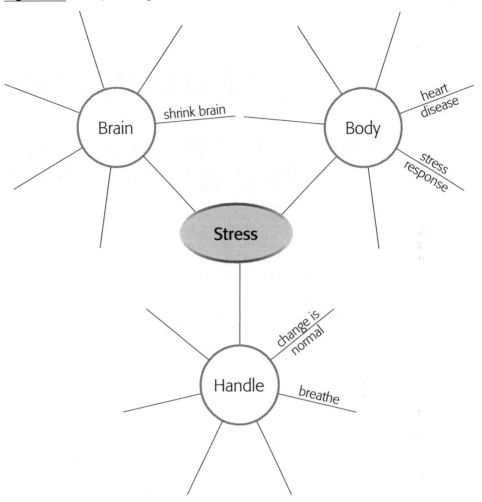

Chapter 5

I Still Want to Know

How Can You Help Students Develop Higher-Order Thinking Skills?

Those ideas and lessons in the last book about helping students develop higher-order thinking skills—especially the lesson plan on Bloom's Taxonomy—were helpful, and I continue to use them. The Common Core State Standards seem to emphasize those higher-order categories, though, and I could use any more ideas I can get. What else do you have?

Higher-order thinking skills are generally considered the ones necessary to apply knowledge you have to a new area and solve problems. In other words, you are able to transfer the facts you know to a situation you have not encountered earlier.

This chapter will focus on five strategies to develop these thinking skills—Bloom's Taxonomy, metacognition, inductive learning, asking questions, what-if thinking, and reflection. It includes engaging lessons that encourage students to want to develop and use these higher-order skills.

Bloom's Taxonomy

Bloom's Taxonomy was developed by a group led by Benjamin Bloom in 1956 to classify thinking into six levels of increasing complexity. A Revised Bloom's Taxonomy was created in 2001 that, among other things, increased its accessibility to students. The changes are not really significant in how teachers and students would apply them, though. The lessons here use the Revised Bloom's, but they can be taught no matter which version you prefer.

The Relevance of Bloom's Taxonomy

This next mini-lesson can be added to the extensive "Bloom's Taxonomy Lesson Plan" in *Helping Students Motivate Themselves* or can be used in any other lesson introducing Bloom's. A simple way for students to begin incorporating what they learn about Bloom's is by using the question starters found in the higher levels of Bloom's (there are countless versions online) when they are demonstrating the reading strategy of asking questions, or if they are watching a video clip and they need to list questions that are coming to mind.

It can also be explained that it's important to learn about Bloom's because, since good readers ask questions, by learning to ask deeper questions students can challenge themselves to dig deeper into the meaning of what they are reading. In addition, learning about Bloom's will help students understand the reasoning behind more challenging class assignments—perhaps there will be fewer groans when the teacher tells students that, in addition to giving the answer to a problem or question, they also have to explain why they chose it!

This next mini-lesson, though, can help students become even more clear about why it is in their self-interest to become familiar with Bloom's Taxonomy and know how to use it in their learning.

Mini-Lesson: Why Is Bloom's Taxonomy Important?

1. The teacher ask students to take three minutes to write down reasons they think knowing Bloom's Taxonomy might be important (this mini-lesson should take place after students have some understanding about the Taxonomy). The teacher can add it's also okay for students to write that they don't think it's important—they just need to write their reasons.

2. The teacher asks students to verbally share in pairs, and asks each group to identify one reason they want to share with the rest of the class. The teacher should explain that they should decide who will say it in one sentence, and that when he or she points at the group, that person should immediately stand up, say it, and then sit down. The teacher explains that he or she wants to move through the groups quickly and writes sentence starters on the whiteboard or overhead:

   > "We think it's important to learn about Bloom's Taxonomy because ..."
   > "We don't think it's important to learn about Bloom's Taxonomy because ..."

The teacher explains that students should pick one or the other—each group says only one sentence.

3. Students quickly say their sentences. If a group says that they do not believe it is important, the teacher should not react negatively.

4. The teacher explains that he or she is going to place a read-aloud on the overhead (Figure 5.1) and read it to students as they read along silently. He or she can then distribute copies to all students. He or she can mention that another reason for learning Bloom's is that, since good readers ask questions, by learning to ask deeper questions students can challenge themselves to dig deeper into the meaning of what they are reading.

5. The teacher says he or she is going to give students five minutes to:

   ♦ Think of a career/job they might be interested in doing in the future.

   ♦ Based on what they know about the career/job now, pick at least two of the Bloom's categories listed in the read-aloud and write an example of how they think they might use those categories in their work. If they are done early, they can think of more examples and/or choose other categories to write about.

   ♦ Students will write their responses in at least two paragraphs using the PQC model: make a Point; Quote from the text supporting your point; make a Comment or a connection to your personal experience, another text, or some other knowledge. The teacher should model an example on the overhead:

      I can see the category of "Create" being important in the work I want to do as a teacher, so I can understand why employers would say that creativity and innovation are skills they want. For example, I would have to create a lesson plan for my students every day.

6. Students write down their responses while the teacher is circulating in the room.

7. Depending on the available time, the teacher can have students verbally share in groups what they wrote, share with the class, and/or turn in their papers to the teacher.

Figure 5.1   Bloom's Taxonomy Read-Aloud

Helps Your Brain Grow Stronger

Research shows that the critical thinking ability developed through using the higher-level thinking skills of Bloom's Taxonomy "strengthens the brain—creating more synapses between nerve cells—just as exercise builds muscle tissue." (1)

"Higher ordering thinking skills … [help] learners make connections between past and new learning, creates new pathways, strengthens existing pathways, and increases the likelihood that the new learning will be consolidated and stored for future retrieval." (2)

Helps You Develop Skills Employers Are Looking For

Survey after survey of employers shows that they are looking to hire people who have the critical thinking skills demonstrated in the higher-levels of Revised Bloom's Taxonomy. They specifically say they want "problem-solving skills rather than memorization of coursework." (3)

Here are a few examples of the skills employers say they want that relate to Bloom's:

CREATE:
"creativity and innovation" (4)

EVALUATE:
"critical thinking" (4)

ANALYZE:
"analytic reasoning" (4)

APPLY:
"apply learning to real world setting" (5)

Sources: (1) Cardellichio & Field (1997), (2) Sousa (2005, p. 259), (3) Slattery (1998), (4) Percentage of employers (n.d.), & (5) Marklein (2008)

Photos and Bloom's

Using photos can be a good way to reinforce an understanding of Bloom's Taxonomy. In an online exercise developed by Learn North Carolina ("A Picture," n.d.), following an introduction to the different levels of Bloom's, students can apply their new knowledge toward developing leveled questions about a photo.

For example, a teacher could use the photo in Figure 5.2, page 96, and model asking questions for each category:

Figure 5.2 Old Photo of Class

Remember: Based on your knowledge and experience, where and when do you think this photo was taken?

Understand: What makes you think it was taken then and there?

Apply: What is a caption you could write for this photo?

Analyze: Reread the caption you wrote. Are there any other possible explanations for what is happening in the photo? Write a different caption for the photo, and then decide which of the two is most likely more accurate and why.

Evaluate: Based on what you know, would a picture of a similar group today be organized the same way? Why or why not?

Create: Suppose you could ask a few people in the photo what they were thinking—what do you think they would say?

The teacher could have several different photos to distribute, along with a sheet of question starters (see the Ed Tech box for free resources) categorized by the Bloom's level to help scaffold the activity. Students could work in pairs to develop their own sequence of questions to share with other small groups or the class. If desired, they could then trade their photos and questions with classmates and answer them. However, answering the questions would not be necessary. This activity is primarily meant to be an engaging way to use a different medium to refresh students' understanding of Bloom's.

Bloom's as Road Map or Compass?

Research suggests that it is not necessarily essential or even beneficial to view Bloom's Taxonomy only as a ladder that must be climbed rung by rung (McLeod, 2012). Of course, some students might require more scaffolding and support than others, but that is the purpose of differentiated instruction.

Though educator Dan Meyer was not specifically referring to Bloom's in this passage from his blog, his point could very easily be applied to the danger of looking at Bloom's as a rigid pyramid:

> **Drills aren't a basketball player's first, only, or most prominent experience with basketball.** Drills come after a student has been sufficiently enticed by *the game of basketball*—either by watching it or playing it on the playground—to sign up for a more dedicated commitment. If a player's first, only, or most prominent experience with basketball is hours of free-throw and perimeter drills, she'll quit the first day—even if she's six foot two with a twenty-eight inch vertical and enormous potential to excel at and love *the game*.
>
> There is a place for drills and explanation in mathematics, as in basketball. But consider what little good they do in either arena if the student isn't *first* made aware of the larger, more enticing purposes they serve. (2012)

After students gain an understanding of Bloom's Taxonomy—through the lesson in *Helping Students Motivate Themselves* or another way—a teacher can show students various representations of the Taxonomy (circle, flower, gears) and have students determine which they think is most accurate (or, even better, create their own!), as well as provide reasons for their judgment. Links to those different illustrations can be found in the Ed Tech box, and can also easily be found by searching "images of Bloom's Taxonomy" on the Web.

Ed Tech
Bloom's Taxonomy Resources

Many Bloom's Taxonomy resources can be found at "The Best Resources For Helping Teachers Use Bloom's Taxonomy In The Classroom" (www.larryferlazzo.edublogs.org/2009/05/25/the-best-resources-for-helping-teachers-use-blooms-taxonomy-in-the-classroom). These materials include links to question starters for different Bloom's levels, as well as to engaging video "mash-ups" demonstrating Bloom's using *The Simpsons, Finding Nemo,* and *Seinfeld*. In addition, the site includes links to illustrations of the different Bloom's levels represented in ways other than its traditional pyramid form.

Metacognition

"To use a fancy word, there's a metacognition deficit. Very few in public life habitually step back and think about the weakness in their own thinking and what they should do to compensate.... Of the problems that afflict the country, this is the underlying one" (Brooks, 2010).

As David Brooks of *The New York Times* writes, metacognition is the action of looking at one's own thinking process. Though there is not always a clear separation between the two, one might consider a cognitive strategy as what you do to arrive at an answer or complete a learning task (for example, connecting a piece of prior knowledge to what you're learning now to better understand it), and a metacognitive strategy as checking to see if there are other ways to do it better (Am I sure the different contexts don't alter its meaning?).

Jon Pratt, a Maine educator, describes cognition and metacognition as a continuum:

"What do I think? —> What other ways can I think? —> What's the best way to think?"

(communication via Twitter to author, August 12, 2012)

According to the Organisation of Economic Co-operation and Development (OECD), students using metacognitive strategies performed nearly two full years above those who did not use them on the Program for International Student Assessment (PISA) test (OECD, 2010).

The National Research Council of the National Academy of Sciences published a report in 2012, "Education for Life and Work: Developing Transferable Knowledge and Skills in the 21st Century" (Pelligrino & Hilton, in press), which highlighted how critical metacognitive capacity is for the ability to transfer existing knowledge to solve new problems (Chapter 6, p. 20). The same report emphasized that metacognitive strategies can indeed be taught and learned (Chapter 6, p. 21).

Teachers modeling their thinking process could be one way to help students develop metacognitive skills, and question-asking "thinking routines" (see the next section in this chapter) could do the same. This lesson plan, as well as the following one, "Asking Questions Lesson Plan," can add to that repertoire of instructional strategies.

Metacognition Lesson Plan

This lesson plan introduces students to the importance of metacognition and how it is shown to increase academic achievement and potentially even brain size. The lesson plan provides concrete strategies that students and teachers can use on an ongoing basis.

There are many immediate actions that teachers can take to help students develop their skills at using metacognitive strategies. However, since they can be most effective after students receive an explicit introduction to metacognition, those ideas are contained within this lesson plan itself at the end under "Subsequent Days."

Instructional Objectives for Students:

- Learn the concept of metacognition and why it is important.

- Read a complex text.

- Develop a repertoire of metacognitive strategies.

- Write a short academic text about metacognition.

Duration: Three sixty-minute periods

Materials:

- Overhead projector or document camera, computer projector, and Internet access

- Highlighters, markers, and construction paper for all students

- Student copies of "Metacognition—I Know (Or Don't Know) That I Know" (Bailey, 2012, www.brainfacts.org/sensing-thinking-behaving/aware-ness-and-attention/articles/2012/metacognition). Note that copies should stop before the "I Believe I Do" subheading, so students will be reading about eighteen very short paragraphs—the first two sections.

- Student copies of Figure 5.3, page 106, and Figure 5.4, page 106

Common Core English Language Arts Standards

Reading: Determine central ideas or themes of a text and analyze their development; summarize the key supporting details and ideas.

Writing: Produce clear and coherent writing in which the development, organization, and style are appropriate to task, purpose, and audience.

Speaking and Listening: Prepare for and participate effectively in a range of conversations and collaborations with diverse partners, building on others' ideas and expressing their own clearly and persuasively.

Language: Demonstrate command of the conventions of standard English grammar and usage when writing or speaking.

Procedure

First Day:

1. Students enter the classroom seeing the word *metacognition* written on the whiteboard or overhead. The teacher points to it, says it, and asks students to repeat it. Next, the teacher does the following exercise, or a comparable one:

    The teachers crunches up a piece of paper, throws it, and intentionally misses a garbage can. The paper falls to the right (of course, students will love that the teacher misses it). The teacher tells the class, "Okay, now I know that I have to adjust my shot. I'm thinking about it, and maybe I need to adjust to the left. I've seen people shoot free throws underhand, so maybe I'll have a better chance if I throw it that way, too, because it would have a higher arc."

    The teacher crunches up another sheet of paper, throws it, and it lands just short, hitting the rim of the can (again, the teacher probably receives great cheers or catcalls from the class). He or she says, "It looks like I'm getting closer. I think I'll just have to throw it a little harder and it should go in."

    The teacher gets another piece of paper and throws it—bull's-eye! He or she says, "Now, the next time I want to try to make a basket here, I'll know to throw it underhand and aim better. That's the kind of thinking I go through on the basketball court, and how we improve in lots of ways. We take the time to think about *why.*

    He or she then tells the class, "Let's see how I do shooting the ball without using metacognition." He quickly crumples up three pieces of paper and just throws them one by one in the direction of the can. None go in. The teacher tells the class, "I'm going to ask a question, and I don't want anyone to call out an answer. Why didn't those three balls go in? Tell a partner." The teacher calls on one student, who probably responds, "Because you didn't think about what you learned from trying it earlier."

    "Exactly," the teacher says. "If we don't 'think about our thinking,' we won't learn from our mistakes or from our successes. We'll always start from scratch when we face a problem. By using metacognition, we'll be able to more effectively apply what we learn now to the future. That's what metacognition is, and that's what we'll be talking about for the next two classes."

2. The teacher explains that the class will be breaking into pairs and reading part of an article titled "Metacognition—I Know (Or Don't Know) That I Know." The teacher tells students that they should take turns reading each paragraph aloud while the other student follows along silently. Students should highlight three to five words in each paragraph that represent the main idea (the teacher should model that in the first paragraph) and write a one-sentence summary for each of the two sections students will be reading. Each group will be given two sheets of construction paper approximately 8.5" x 3" and will write in large letters the summary sentences for each section. In addition, students should annotate the article to show at least one example of making a connection to their personal experiences or to another text; evaluating (picking something they like or don't like/agree or disagree with) and giving a reason; and visualizing (drawing a picture). Students will get twenty minutes to complete the assignment.

3. Students break into pairs and are given highlighters, construction sheets, markers, and copies of the article. The teacher circulates while students are reading.

4. The class comes back together. The teacher asks two students to share what they wrote as their connections and then does the same for evaluating and visualizing. It's always fun to invite students to show their drawings on the document camera for the class to see.

5. Next, the teacher asks several students to share their summary sentences for the two sections. He or she then collects them and explains that they will be placed on the classroom wall. He or she explains that students should keep the article because they will be using it tomorrow.

6. On the overhead, the teacher points out the brain scan images in the article, which show where people who use metacognitive strategies have more brain volume. He or she says that, as the article states, researchers don't know if that's because using metacognition increases brain size or if people who use more metacognition start out with a larger amount. But, the teacher continues, it's clear that it certainly won't hurt your brain if you use more metacognition.

7. The teacher explains that the class is going to begin learning some specific metacognitive strategies that they can use. For now, though, he or she wants to share a brief PISA read-aloud (Figure 5.3). The teacher explains that the PISA is a test taken by students from many, many countries around the world, including here in the United States, and is commonly used to evaluate school systems in different countries.

8. The teacher puts the read-aloud on the overhead, and asks students to read it silently as he or she reads it to the class. He or she repeats the portion that says students who use metacognitive strategies like the ones

mentioned in the report do academic work a full two years above students who do not use them. The teacher then passes out copies and asks students to keep them with the article.

9. The teacher asks students to think silently for a minute about what kind of metacognitive strategies they use to help them learn. He or she can prompt students to think about some of the things they did when they were reading the article. The teacher asks student to write down these strategies and then verbally share with a partner. The teacher then calls on students to share with the class and writes responses on the overhead. As the list gets bigger, he or she can affirm that students are using metacognitive strategies now, and that tomorrow they will talk about these and more. (Important note: This activity should be done during the first day. If time is running out, delay the PISA read-aloud until the following day.)

10. If there is still time, the teacher can ask students to take a minute to write down what they thought was the most important or interesting thing they learned today and get into groups of three to verbally share them. The teacher can then call on some students to share with the class.

11. Afterward, the teacher can put the construction paper summaries on the wall throughout the room in six distinct areas. In other words, perhaps eight strips in one corner, another eight near a window, another in another corner, etc.

Second Day:

1. Students count off numbers one through six to form six groups. The teacher explains that he or she is going to assign each number group a section of the construction paper strips from yesterday. Each student has to write one summary sentence from the assigned area/wall that he or she likes and why. When the teacher yells "Switch!" each group will move to the next section on the right and repeat the assignment. They will get only two minutes at each section, so they will have to read and write quickly.

2. Students take a piece of paper and hard surface (a book or a notebook) to write on and complete the process.

3. The teacher gets everyone back to their seats and calls on a few students to share just one summary sentence they wrote down and their reason for liking it. The teacher then explains that not only did this activity serve as a refresher of yesterday's work but that it was also an example of their using metacognition by having to think about why they liked the sentences they wrote down. Now, they'll be able to compare in their minds what they had written a day earlier for their summary sentences and how they could have written it differently.

4. The activity described in this step—a student survey—is adapted with permission (Askell-Williams, Lawson, & Skrzypiec, 2012).

The teacher explains that he or she is going to review a list of metacognitive strategies (some of them might be cognitive strategies but, since there is often overlap between the two and since it's not important to differentiate between the two for this lesson—the point, after all, is to make students more aware of how they learn—teachers can call them all metacognitive). The teacher explains he or she is going to put a list on the overhead and give students a copy of a metacognitive strategy survey (Figure 5.4). He or she is going to read each item and briefly comment on it. After that, he or she wants students to circle the word or phrase that most accurately says how often they use the strategy: never, sometimes, often, or all the time. He or she explains that students will not be graded on this survey, that they will be the only people who see it, and that it's important that they be honest. Being honest will help them become better learners. (Note: If a teacher wants to make this lesson into an action research project, he or she can collect the surveys at the end of class and make copies before returning them the next day to students, explaining to students that the data will be used only to help him or her learn to become a better teacher for them.)

The teacher distributes the sheets, reminding students not to complete them until after they review each strategy as a class, and verbally goes through the list. After saying each strategy, the teacher should give a quick example. The teacher can explain that students should primarily think about what they do in this class, but they should also remember that it's important to use metacognitive strategies in other classes and in learning outside of school. If a strategy was mentioned the previous day, the teacher should refer to it as one mentioned by students. If students mentioned a useful strategy that is not already on the survey, the teacher should add it.

This process should take fifteen to twenty minutes.

5. The teacher says that students should now pick two strategies on the list that they did not mark as using very often and that they want to start using more. The teacher will give them 11" x 14" paper to write them down (it can be just a phrase like "Plan time better so I don't rush") and illustrate each one. At the bottom of each poster students should write what they are going to do to remind themselves about these two strategies (for example, keep the survey list in the front of their binder). The teacher should model a simple poster that he or she created.

6. Students are given the rest of the period to create their posters. If they are not done, the teacher can assign them as homework for the next day. The teacher should remind students to keep all their materials—the article and read-aloud from yesterday and the survey today—because they will need them the next day.

Third Day:

1. The teacher explains that students will be showing their posters and explaining them verbally to their classmates. They will do it in a "speed-dating" style—half the class will turn their desks around, facing another classmate. They will get one minute each to show and explain their poster, including what they are going to do to remind themselves to use the strategy. At the end of two minutes, the teacher will yell "Switch!" and one row of students will move to the next person. During this process students should have a pen and paper to write down ideas they like that other students share about reminding themselves.

2. This process goes on for twenty to thirty minutes. It is not necessary for *everyone* to share with each student.

3. The teacher brings the class together and calls on students to share the best "reminder methods" they heard. The teacher makes a list on the overhead.

4. The teacher says that students are now going to answer a question by writing a paragraph in the ABC format (Answer the question; Back it up with a quote or other evidence; make a Connection to an experience or another text). The question is: "What is the most important thing you have learned about metacognition over the last three days?"

   If students are not familiar with this kind of paragraph, the teacher can show a model from one of the other chapters. Students can use quotations from the article, read-aloud, or survey.

5. Students are given twenty minutes to write their paragraphs, and then are asked to share them verbally with a partner.

6. The teacher collects paragraphs and posters from students, and hangs up posters on the wall afterward to serve as reminders.

Subsequent Days:

It is important for the teacher to continually reinforce student use of meta-cognitive strategies. One way is for the teacher to model his or her thinking process. Another is to ask questions using thinking routines (see the next section in this chapter). Teachers can also regularly remind students of what they wrote on their posters. Students can be periodically asked at the end of class to write what metacognitive strategies they used that day and when they used them. Finally, the researchers who developed the student survey used in this lesson recommend that teachers integrate several questions regularly in their teaching to reinforce students' use of metacognitive strategies. Some of these questions are:

- What is the topic for today's lesson?
- What will be important ideas in today's lesson?
- What do you already know about this topic?
- What can you relate this to?
- What will you do to remember the key ideas?
- Is there anything about this topic you don't understand or are not clear about?

(Askell-Williams, et al., 2012, p. 425)

Assessment

- The ABC paragraph can be easily assessed for understanding.

- If desired, teachers could develop their own rubrics for use with this activity. See "The Best Rubric Sites (And A Beginning Discussion About Their Use)" (www.larryferlazzo.edublogs.org/2010/09/18/the-best-rubric-sites-and-a-beginning-discussion-about-their-use) for multiple free online tools for creating rubrics.

Possible Extensions

- Once each month or once each quarter, students could evaluate themselves on if they are increasing their use of particular metacognitive strategies and if they want to work on others.

- Students could create short humorous skits portraying the use of metacognitive strategies. They could, but would not necessarily have to be, videotaped for posting online.

- The teacher could periodically take photos of students individually or in groups and have students immediately write what metacognitive strategy they were using during that class activity. Shortly afterward, the teacher could post them on a class blog and have students type in what they wrote as a sort of "metacognitive caption" (Anderson, 2012).

Ed Tech
Online Video

It is easy to videotape a student performance with a smart phone (though it is generally a good idea to get a very inexpensive microphone accessory for better sound) and automatically upload it to YouTube (and it is equally easy to incorporate your preferred privacy settings). Before posting student performances online—or, in fact, any student photo or even work examples—it is important to obtain parent permission. See "The Best Teacher Resources For Online Student Safety & Legal Issues" (www.larryferlazzo.edublogs. org/2009/08/10/the-best-teacher-resources-for-online-student-safety-legal-issues).

Figure 5.3   PISA Read-Aloud

Students who use appropriate strategies to understand and remember what they read, such as underlining important parts of the texts or discussing what they read with other people, perform at least 73 points higher in the PISA assessment— … nearly two full school years—than students who use these strategies the least. (OECD, 2010, p. 13)

Figure 5.4   Metacognitive Strategy Survey

(Many of the items in this survey are have been adapted from Askell-Williams, Lawson, & Skrzypiec, 2012, http://www.springerlink.com/content/p068qm6808q5g075/, p. 418. Used with permission.)

1.   I visualize images in my mind, draw pictures, or draw diagrams to help me understand what we are studying.

Never   Sometimes   Often   All the Time

2.   I think of questions that I try to answer about what we are studying.

Never   Sometimes   Often   All the Time

3.   When I am studying something new in class, I think back to what I already know about it, including what I have read in other texts.

Never   Sometimes   Often   All the Time

(continued)

Figure 5.4 Metacognitive Strategy Survey (*continued*)

4. I talk with others about what I am studying in class.

   Never   Sometimes   Often   All the Time

5. I think about experiences I can connect to what I'm studying, and remember what has helped me in the past and what has not helped me.

   Never   Sometimes   Often   All the Time

6. When I don't understand something we are studying, I review it again.

   Never   Sometimes   Often   All the Time

7. I make lists of things that I don't understand very well in class, so that I can follow up later by reading more or talking to other people about those things.

   Never   Sometimes   Often   All the Time

8. When I have finished an activity in class, I go back to double-check my work.

   Never   Sometimes   Often   All the Time

9. I organize my time to manage my learning in class.

   Never   Sometimes   Often   All the Time

10. I make plans for how to do the activities in class before I start working on the assignment.

    Never   Sometimes   Often   All the Time

11. Before I give an answer, I think about how others might answer the question. In other words, I look at both sides of an issue.

    Never   Sometimes   Often   All the Time

12. I highlight or underline important words in a passage.

    Never   Sometimes   Often   All the Time

13. I try to predict what might happen next when I am reading or trying to solve a problem in class.

    Never   Sometimes   Often   All the Time

Asking Questions

Teachers can help students develop and use thinking routines to get beyond the surface of issues. One such routine was developed by Project Zero at Harvard and consists of a relatively simple formula—the teacher regularly asking, "What's going on here?" and, after a student response, continuing with, "What do you see that makes you say so?" (Perkins, 2003, para. 7).

The lessons in this chapter, however, are designed to help *students* develop *their* capacity to ask deeper questions, as well as to help them understand the reasoning behind doing more and more intellectually challenging class assignments.

Asking questions is an art that requires much skill and practice. As discussed in the first chapter, self-efficacy can be a big part of intrinsic motivation. The more we emphasize the importance of asking good questions, and the more we can help students develop the skills to do so and help them see why that capacity is important in their lives, the greater the chance of their actually doing so.

This next lesson plan (parts of which have been adapted with permission from one created by literacy consultant Kelly Young at Pebble Creek Labs, www.pebblecreeklabs.com) is just one more tool to help that process along.

Asking Questions Lesson Plan

Instructional Objectives for Students:

- Learn more ways to ask higher-level questions and reasons why it is important to have that skill.

- Practice public-speaking skills.

- Further develop ability to respond to "on-demand" writing tasks.

Duration: Three sixty-minute class periods

Materials:

- Overhead projector or document camera, computer projector, and access to the Internet

- Student copies of Figure 5.5, page 115, and Figure 5.6, page 116 (Note: Figure 5.6 can be used, but it would be better for the teacher to use it as a model to create his or her own read-alouds related to a current unit of study.)

- Student copies of Bloom's Taxonomy Questions Starters (www.larryferlazzo. edublogs.org/2009/05/25/the-best-resources-for-helping-teachers-use-blooms-taxonomy-in-the-classroom)

- Student copies of Figure 5.7, page 118

Common Core English Language Arts Standards

Reading: Determine central ideas or themes of a text and analyze their development; summarize the key supporting details and ideas.

Writing: Produce clear and coherent writing in which the development, organization, and style are appropriate to task, purpose, and audience.

Speaking and Listening: Prepare for and participate effectively in a range of conversations and collaborations with diverse partners, building on others' ideas and expressing their own clearly and persuasively.

Language: Demonstrate command of the conventions of standard English grammar and usage when writing or speaking.

Procedure

First Day:

1. The teacher begins by saying the class is going to learn about asking good questions today, and immediately shows his or her choice of one or two videos at "The Best Videos Showing The Importance Of Asking Good Questions" (www.larryferlazzo.edublogs.org/2012/08/04/the-best-videos-showing-the-importance-of-asking-good-questions-help-me-find-more).

2. The teacher explains that the class has already spent time learning about Bloom's Taxonomy (assuming those lessons have already been done) and that students have learned how asking good questions when they are reading helps them dig deeper into the text. The teacher continues by saying that there are other reasons to ask good questions, too. The videos showed some examples. There are others: you want to be able to ask good questions of your doctor; job interviewers not only want to ask you questions, but they want to see if *you* can ask good ones, too.

3. The teacher places Figure 5.5 on the overhead and tells students to read along silently while he or she reads it to them. He or she reads the quotations on the sheet, and then gives students the following assignment (it should also be posted on the overhead):

   o Students will be assigned one quotation each, and they also will choose their favorite from the remaining ones.

   o They will have to write a paragraph about each quotation, for a total of two paragraphs.

   o Each paragraph will follow the same model:

   ⊙ It will start with the quotation: _____ said, " _____
   _____."

   ⊙ I think that means _____.

   ⊙ This reminds me of (a personal experience or information from another text or other source).

4. The teacher gives each student a copy of the read-aloud and says they will get fifteen minutes to complete the assignment. Students begin writing while the teacher circulates and identifies students to call on to share their paragraphs with the class afterward.

5. At the end of fifteen minutes, the teacher tells students to break into partners and read one of their paragraphs to the other student. The other student is to then ask a question that cannot be answered with a yes or a no. The teacher models potential question starters and/or refers students to a Bloom's Taxonomy question starter sheet students have (see earlier section in this chapter) or a list of question starters that might be posted on the classroom wall.

6. The teacher then calls on two or three selected students to come up and share their paragraphs on the overhead.

7. The teacher then collects student paragraphs.

8. The next section of the lesson plan focuses on literal and interpretative questions, and is adapted from a lesson developed by literacy consultant Kelly Young.

   The teacher asks the class, "What color are my shoes?" The class responds, and then the teacher asks, "How many hands do I have?" and the class responds again. The teacher explains that questions like these are *literal* and writes that word on the whiteboard or overhead. Under the word, the teacher writes "right there" and explains that this is another word to call such questions—right-there questions. He or she asks the class, "Why do you think they're called right-there questions?" The class probably will respond, "Because the answers are right there!"

   Next, the teacher asks the class, "What kind of mood do you think I'm in today?" Some people in the class might respond, and the teacher can ask them why they think that. Then the teacher can ask, "What can you tell about me by the kind of clothes I wear?" Some students will respond, and, again, the teacher can ask them why they think that (all these questions and answers can be done in a spirit of fun). The teacher explains that these kinds of questions are *interpretative* and writes that word on the board. Under it, he or she writes "think about." He or she asks the class, "Why do you think they're called think-about questions?" The class probably will respond, "Because you have to think about the answers!"

9. The teacher tells students that they will be talking more about literal and interpretative questions in the next class. If there is time left, he or she could have students think of one literal and one interpretative question to ask about themselves (similar to the ones the teacher just asked) and share it with a partner. The partner needs to answer the questions and say if he or she thinks they are indeed literal and interpretative questions. The teacher gives students one minute to think about the questions before students share. If there is still time afterward, the teacher can ask some students to share their questions with the class.

Second Day:

1. The teacher reminds students that they studied literal and interpretative questions the previous day. He or she asks each student to turn to a nearby student and say the other terms used to describe the two types of questions. The teacher then asks the class to share so that everyone is reminded that they can also be called right-there and think-about questions.

2. The teacher explains that, obviously, think-about questions are the harder ones, and that those are the ones students want to get better at asking. Those are the questions that will get the important answers you need from a doctor, from the police, or from someone interviewing you for a job. Those are the kinds of questions you should be asking yourself when you are reading, and the ones you should be asking your teachers. And those are the kinds of questions your teachers should be asking you—most of the time. The teacher emphasizes that literal questions have their place and purpose. However, the teacher says, we should all be asking more interpretative questions than literal ones.

   The teacher asks the students which questions they think are more interesting—literal or interpretative? In other words, which is more interesting—to find out the color of my shoes, or to find out what kind of mood I'm in? Students will probably respond that they think interpretative questions are more interesting. The teacher can explain another reason students and teachers should ask more interpretative questions: studies have found that we tend to remember more from finding out information from questions we find interesting (Kang et al., n.d., p. 3). The teacher can also point out that asking interesting questions comes in handy when you want people to like you—for example, if you're on a date, spending time with friends, or just trying to meet new people. A recent study found that the reward areas of the brain become active when a person is talking about himself or herself. *Time* magazine described the study's conclusions this way: "Humans get a biochemical buzz from self-disclosure" (Luscombe, 2012).

3. The teacher explains that the class is going to practice asking questions today. The teacher places the first read-aloud from Figure 5.6 on the overhead, asks students to read silently with him or her, and then reads it aloud.

4. The teacher shows and reads the literal question and asks students to answer. He or she then shows the interpretative question and points out that you have to think about the answer. He or she does not have to have students answer each question, since the point of the lesson is to develop students' question-asking skills. However, the teacher could certainly have students answer some or all of them.

5. The teacher repeats the exercise with the second read-aloud.

6. The teacher reads the third read-aloud, as well as the interpretative question, but then distributes copies and has students take a minute to write their own literal questions and then share with a partner. The teacher then calls on one or two students to share their questions.

7. The teacher then distributes the fourth read-aloud and gives students two to three minutes to write both a literal and an interpretative question. He or

she should also remind students to take out their Bloom's Taxonomy question starters (if they have them from a previous lesson) or should distribute copies. He or she can explain that the two lowest levels are generally literal and the upper levels are generally interpretative. The teacher can also say that literal and interpretative are just another way to categorize questions, and may be a little easier to remember than all the Bloom's levels. If students have not learned about Bloom's yet, the teacher can still distribute the question starters and say that Bloom's is just another way to categorize questions, that the class will study it at a later time, and, that for now they can just use the question starters to help them formulate their literal and interpretative questions. Students write their questions, share them with a partner, and then the teacher identifies a few to share with the class.

8. The teacher then gives both the fifth and sixth read-alouds to students and repeats the process. (The teacher can also choose to use fewer read-alouds in this part of the lesson.)

9. Next, the teacher announces that in small groups of three people, students will prepare and perform a skit that should last no longer than two or three minutes. They will need to create a situation where asking interpretative questions will benefit them. The teacher places Figure 5.7 on the overhead and reviews it. The teacher can choose how he or she wants to assign group members—by student choice, by counting off, or by the teacher strategically creating groups. The teacher explains that each group should first identify their first three choices of scenarios. They can number them in order of priority and bring them up to the teacher, who will choose which of the three they will perform (this way not every group can pick the same situation).

10. If there is time, groups can begin their work. If not, they can start the next day.

Third Day:

1. Students are given fifteen minutes to practice their performance.

2. The teacher explains that during each skit, members of the audience should write the first names of members (or at least the name of one member) of each group and what they think is the best interpretative question that was asked by that group. After each performance, one member of the group will call on one audience member to share what he or she wrote down as the best question. (Note: An alternative to having each group perform for the entire class, which would take up a substantial amount of time, would be to have groups of three groups. In other words, if there were nine small groups, three of them could each be placed in different sections of the classroom, and then each group would perform for two other groups.)

Each group performs. The teacher could choose to briefly highlight particular questions or performances. Afterward, the teacher collects notes students took during the performances.

The teacher now explains that students need to write an ABC paragraph (Answer the question; Back it up with a quote or other evidence; make a Connection to an experience or another text) answering this question: "Is it important to be able to ask interpretative questions? If so, why?" The teacher can explain the evidence students cite could be a quotation from the first day's sheet or examples from the skits they performed and watched.

3. Students are given fifteen minutes to complete the paragraphs. If there is time, they can then verbally share them with partners and turn the paragraphs in to the teacher.

Assessment

- The first day's paragraph and the ABC paragraph can be easily assessed for understanding.

- Audience notes and the performance qualities will also be a clear indication of student attention.

- If desired, teachers could develop their own rubrics for use with this activity. See "The Best Rubric Sites (And A Beginning Discussion About Their Use)" (www.larryferlazzo.edublogs.org/2010/09/18/the-best-rubric-sites-and-a-beginning-discussion-about-their-use) for multiple free online tools for creating rubrics.

Possible Extensions

- Student performances could be videotaped and posted online (see earlier Ed Tech tip in this chapter for details).

- Students could research and develop their own read-alouds with literal and interpretative questions they teach to classmates.

- Teachers could follow up this lesson at a later date with mini-lessons on additional techniques designed to help students develop question-asking skills. You can find information on methods like the Question Formulation Technique, Connect Extend Challenge, and others at www.larryferlazzo.edublogs.org/2012/05/23/the-best-posts-articles-about-asking-good-questions-help-me-find-more.

Figure 5.5 Asking Questions Read-Aloud

"Judge a man by his questions rather than by his answers."

—Voltaire, philosopher and writer in 18th-century France

"My mother made me a scientist without ever intending to. Every other Jewish mother in Brooklyn would ask her child after school: So? Did you learn anything today? But not my mother. 'Izzy,' she would say, 'did you ask a good question today?' That difference—asking good questions—made me become a scientist."

—Isidor Isaac Rabi, winner of the Nobel Prize in Physics

"Sometimes questions are more important than answers."

—Nancy Willard, American poet and writer

"If they can get you asking the wrong questions, they don't have to worry about answers."

—Thomas Pynchon, author

"The most common source of management mistakes is not the failure to find the right answers. It is the failure to ask the right questions."

—Peter Drucker, financial writer

"He explained to me with great insistence that every question possessed a power that did not lie in the answer."

—Elie Wiesel, writer and concentration camp survivor

"History can come in handy. If you were born yesterday, with no knowledge of the past, you might easily accept whatever the government tells you. But knowing a bit of history—while it would not absolutely prove the government was lying in a given instance—might make you skeptical, lead you to ask questions, make it more likely that you would find out the truth."

—Howard Zinn, historian

"Schooling, instead of encouraging the asking of questions, too often discourages it."

—Madeleine L'Engle, author

Figure 5.6   Practice Read-Aloud

Read-Aloud One: Chinese records claim that a Chinese monk named Huishen traveled 7,000 miles east of China. The monk then landed in a country he called Fusang. Some people say Fusang was California.

Literal Question: What was the name of the Chinese monk?

Interpretative Question: What do you think the Native Americans would have thought of the monk?

Read-Aloud Two: In the 1850s the United States allowed only whites to become citizens. Chinese immigrants were not allowed to vote. They also could not own land. Chinese people could also not testify against whites in court.

Literal Question: What were the Chinese not allowed to own?

Interpretative Question: Imagine you were a Chinese immigrant who had been shot by a white person. How would you have felt if you could not testify against that person in court?

Read-Aloud Three: After news of the discovery of gold in California reached China in 1849, there was an increase in Chinese immigrants to the West Coast of the United States. They came because wars, floods, and famine had made it difficult to earn a living in China.

Literal Question: _____

Interpretative Question: How do you think the Chinese heard about the discovery of gold?

Read-Aloud Four: Chinese workers on the railroad ate a traditional diet including dried oysters, dried fish, sweet rice, crackers, dried bamboo, salted cabbage, sugar, dried fruits and vegetables, dried seaweed, Chinese bacon, dried mushrooms, tea, rice, pork, and chicken. This was a much healthier diet than the beef, beans, bread, butter, and potatoes of white workers at the time. The Chinese also drank a large amount of hot tea. White workers, instead, would drink cold water. This water was often contaminated and caused illness among the workers.

Literal Question: _____

Interpretative Question: _____

_____

(continued)

Figure 5.6   Practice Read-Aloud (*continued*)

Read-Aloud Five: Chinese workers on the railroad worked six days a week from sunrise to sundown. They were paid $1 each day. Three thousand Chinese people were hired to work on the railroad.

In 1867, two thousand Chinese workers went on strike. They demanded a raise to $40 each month. The strike ended in one week, and the Chinese workers were forced to go back to work without a raise in their pay.

Literal Question: _____

Interpretative Question: _____

_____

Read-Aloud Six: The typical Chinese gold seeker was male, in his late teens or early twenties, single, and had not been to school. His goal was to return to China as soon as he had earned a lot of money, and he continued to follow Chinese traditions in areas including clothing, language, and food. He stayed in places where there were other Chinese people. The largest and most important of these communities was San Francisco's Chinatown.

Literal Question: _____

Interpretative Question: _____

_____

Figure 5.7   Question-Asking Skit Assignment

You will work in groups of three (except if you choose the situation described in number nine—then you can be in a group of four) to prepare and perform a skit that should last no longer than two or three minutes. You will need to create a situation where asking interpretative questions will benefit you and should ask as many questions as possible—at least five and preferably more. For example, you could be:

1. in a classroom where asking interpretative questions is helping you learn more

2. interviewed for a job by two people who are asking if you have any questions about the position

3. in a doctor's office with a family member who has just received a diagnosis, and you are trying to find out more information

4. interviewed by two college admissions officers who are asking if you have any questions

5. in a public meeting where a business owner and a city official want to put an industrial plant that will burn toxic waste in your neighborhood

6. helping a friend who has fallen on hard times go to the Department of Social Services to see what kind of housing, food, and child-care support the county and state could provide

7. a parent who is encouraging your two children to develop their imagination by creating a story

8. interviewing family members for a family history you are writing for your parents as a present

9. on a double date wanting to make a good impression

10. in a different situation of your choosing that must be approved by the teacher

You must decide on your first three choices and send one person to the teacher with them. The teacher will then pick one to make sure that not all students choose the same situation.

At the beginning of your performance, you should explain what situation you chose. You may have simple props and must keep things appropriate and respectful. Also, have fun with it!

Self-Driven Learning: Teaching Strategies for Student Motivation

Inductive Learning

Inductive learning uses the brain's natural inclination to seek and generate patterns to guide it toward the higher levels of Bloom's Taxonomy (Washburn, 2012). Generally, teaching and learning inductively means that students are provided with examples that they categorize and then use those classifications to create concepts or rules. The use of the data set (a series of passages or pieces of information that need to be categorized) in Chapter 4's "Stress Lesson Plan" is one example of how inductive learning might look in the classroom.

Teaching *deductively*, in contrast, can mean giving students concepts or rules first and then having them practice applying them.

The steps in using a data set can be fairly clear. First, students reach each item in the data set and annotate it, typically with reading strategies. Students next classify the examples (individually or with partners), being sure to highlight or underline their evidence for determining that each belongs in that specific category. They might use categories given to them by the teacher or ones they determine themselves. Then, they might add new pieces of data they find, and/or they may convert their categories into paragraphs and simple essays. They might also just stop at the categorization process.

The evidence supporting the effectiveness of inductive learning and teaching continues to grow. As mentioned earlier, a 2011 meta-analysis of hundreds of studies found that "enhanced discovery learning" was a more effective form of teaching than either "direct instruction" or "unassisted discovery learning" (Marzano, 2011). The researcher's definition of enhanced discovery learning is almost how a textbook would describe the inductive process.

Text data sets can be used to inductively teach and learn in just about any subject and lesson. The next lesson plan provides just one more example—using a text data set to help students learn correct punctuation. It was inspired by a lesson taught and written about by educator Elizabeth Schlessman (2011) in *Rethinking Schools* magazine. The text data set used is designed for early English language learners, but the content and lesson objectives can easily be modified. The inductive learning process described, however, is a fairly typical one and can be applied to any subject or topic. It is similar to the lesson plan on stress in Chapter 4, though that activity was designed to also provide scaffolding for students to write an essay—inductive learning can be used for many purposes!

This kind of inductive learning can be especially effective if students have previously done the lesson on metacognition. There are many opportunities in an inductive lesson plan to make explicit connections between the two, and to help students remember that though the *content* of the lesson is important, the thinking *process* they are using is equally important over the long-term. Remembering this interconnectedness can result in greater student engagement and self-motivation.

Learning Punctuation Inductively Lesson Plan

Instructional Objectives for Students: Students will identify and apply rules to use punctuation correctly.

Duration: One sixty-minute class period

Materials:

- Overhead or document camera

- Student copies of Figure 5.8, page 124, or a more challenging teacher-created data set if students are more English proficient

- Small poster paper for all students, along with glue, scissors, highlighters, and markers

Common Core English Language Arts Standards

Writing: Produce clear and coherent writing in which the development, organization, and style are appropriate to task, purpose, and audience.

Speaking and Listening: Prepare for and participate effectively in a range of conversations and collaborations with diverse partners, building on others' ideas and expressing their own clearly and persuasively.

Language: Demonstrate command of the conventions of standard English grammar and usage when writing or speaking.

Procedure

First Day:

1. The teacher announces the class is going to be doing something different with punctuation today. He or she shows one or both of the videos at "The Best Resources On Punctuation" (www.larryferlazzo.edublogs.org/2012/08/06/the-best-resources-on-punctuation).

2. The teacher explains that instead of just telling students what to learn, he or she is going to give them some material so they can try to figure it out on their own—it will be like a puzzle. He or she places Figure 5.8 on the overhead and explains that students will work with partners to put the items into categories. As an example, the teacher could read numbers six and nine and ask students what the two have in common. After students reply

that they are both questions and end in a question mark, the teacher can highlight the question mark and copy the two sentences on the whiteboard under a category label of "Question Mark (?)"

The teacher explains that students will work with partners to identify several categories, cut out the sentences and glue them under the category names, and highlight the clue words (the evidence) that they are using to justify their choices. Each category should be the name of a punctuation mark, and it's possible that some sentences could fit in more than one. In that case, students need to write a sentence explaining why they chose to put it where they did. The teacher tells students they should make sure to leave space for more sentences under each category.

The teacher explains that this process is called inductive learning. The brain naturally wants to see and find patterns, and that is what students will be doing—looking for patterns. He or she explains that research shows we learn better by doing this instead of just listening to someone tell us facts.

The teacher then distributes copies of the data set, glue, poster paper, and scissors to students. Students can work in pairs, but each student needs to make his or her own poster. The teacher explains that students will have twenty-five minutes to complete their posters and that they should make sure they include the number of each sentence on the poster, too.

3. Students work on the data set while the teacher circulates throughout the classroom.

4. After about fifteen minutes, the teacher should identify a student who has correctly put a few sentences into a category. The teacher tells that student that he or she is going to call on him or her in a minute just to give the sentence numbers in one category—without saying what category. The teacher then asks students to stop working for a minute and has the chosen student call out the numbers in one of his or her categories. The teacher writes the numbers on the whiteboard and asks students to take thirty seconds to figure out what category fits those numbers. He or she then calls on one student to say the category, and asks the original student if that category is correct or not. This entire interruption should not take more than ninety seconds, and then the teacher can tell students to return to their work. The teacher might or might not want to repeat this activity in another five minutes.

5. At the end of the allotted time (twenty-five minutes), the teacher combines student pairs into groups of four and asks the pairs to compare their categories. After a minute, the teacher can ask if there were any disagreements and, if so, lead a short class discussion about them. The key issue is if students have *evidence* backing up their positions.

6. The teacher then tells students that they will again go back to working in their pairs to write a sentence for each category explaining the rule that governs its use. The teacher can model an example for the question mark category: "You write a question mark after a sentence that seeks information." He or she tells students to write their sentences next to the title of each category, and that they will have five minutes to complete them all.

7. After five minutes, the teacher puts students into groups of four again (the same student pairs can stay together, but the makeup of each group of four should change) and tells them to share their explanations.

8. The teacher brings the class back together and calls on one student per category to share his or her rule with the class.

9. The teacher then tells students that they need to write three of their own example sentences for each category. If there is time available, students can work on them in class. If not, it will be homework.

10. Students turn in their completed posters at the end of class or the next day, and the teacher can post them on the classroom walls as punctuation reminders.

Assessment

- The completed poster can be easily used for assessment.

- If desired, teachers could develop their own rubrics for use with this activity. See "The Best Rubric Sites (And A Beginning Discussion About Their Use)" (www.larryferlazzo.edublogs.org/2010/09/18/the-best-rubric-sites-and-a-beginning-discussion-about-their-use) for multiple free online tools for creating rubrics.

Possible Extensions

- Students can turn the explanations of punctuation rules into illustrated posters.

- Students can go to the computer lab or use classroom laptops or tablets to practice using correct punctuation online at "The Best Resources On Punctuation" (www.larryferlazzo.edublogs.org/2012/08/06/the-best-resources-on-punctuation).

- Students can create an online picture data set (see the Ed Tech box on the next page) to illustrate sentences they develop or to add on to the given text examples.

Ed Tech
Online Practice

The Internet is awash with free activities that students can use to practice and reinforce knowledge learned in the classroom, like the punctuation sites found at the link on page 122. I have compiled over a thousand "The Best of" lists on just about every imaginable classroom topic ("My Best of Series," at www.larryferlazzo.edublogs.org/about/my-best-of-series). They can be used in a trip to the computer lab or by students if you have a laptop or tablet cart; they can be used as homework ("The Best Sites that Students can use Independently And Let Teachers Check On Progress," at www.larryferlazzo.edublogs. org/2008/05/21/the-best-sites-that-students-can-use-independently-and-let-teachers-check-on-progress); or they can be used by students who finish an assignment early.

Ed Tech
Picture Data Sets

Students can create picture data sets online to supplement many classroom inductive learning activities. Using the categories they have chosen, students can grab images off the Web or upload their own photos of items that fit into those same categories. These photos can either illustrate text students have already identified in class or new ones, and they then can label them with words or sentences. They could also mix up their images, list the names of categories, and challenge other students to organize them correctly. There are several easy and free online tools that allow students to mix and match images for these kinds of activities, found at "The Best Online Virtual 'Corkboards' (or 'Bulletin Boards')" (www.larryferlazzo.edublogs.org/2011/03/30/the-best-online-virtual-corkboards-or-bulletin-boards).

Figure 5.8   Punctuation Data Set

1. The sky is so beautiful!
2. Lorena likes to sing.
3. "Please give me money," said Sia.
4. Marco has candy, a pencil, and books in his backpack.
5. Marco yelled, "Goal!"
6. How are you?
7. January, February, March, and April are months of the year.
8. "Please give me candy!" cried Hiram.
9. Did the car turn right or left?
10. Abi said, "You are the best teacher in the world."
11. Eduar kicked the soccer ball, ran to the goal, and fell down.
12. "I got an A on the test," said Francisco.
13. Is Mr. Ferlazzo handsome or ugly?
14. Mr. Ferlazzo went to the cabinet, got candy, and threw it to the students.
15. Duy is silly.
16. "I love this class!" yelled Ma.
17. Sunday, Monday, Tuesday, Wednesday, Thursday, Friday, and Saturday are the days of the week.

What–If Thinking

Another engaging way to help students develop higher-order thinking skills is through what-if thinking activities. Imagining one moment in history changing (What if George Washington had died at Valley Forge?) and exploring the possible consequences reminds us that history is a series of causes and effects and not necessarily predetermined. Such exercises can help students gain a greater grasp of the fragility, interconnections, and imponderables that we have confronted in our past and will face in our future.

And, even more importantly, as *New York Times* science writer James Gorman (2012) suggests, "the value of speculation would be to see if it prompts more research, ... more study." Reimagining the world in a strategically designed lesson like the one in this section can provoke students to revisit what they thought they had previously learned in order to construct a logical alternative.

This kind of what-if thinking, however, does not have to be limited to studies of history. It can be used to promote a similar level of engagement in literature by having students explore their choices of what-if questions (For *Of Mice and Men,* for example: "What would have happened if Lennie had not killed Curley's wife?"). And, of course, speculative thinking plays a key role in any kind of science instruction.

A writer in *The Wall Street Journal* even partially credits the Montessori education system and its development of a what-if awareness for the success some of the most innovative companies and organizations in the world today, including Google, Amazon, and Wikipedia (Sims, 2011).

This next lesson plan, inspired by the work of educators Diana Laufenberg and Carla Federman (Ferlazzo, 2012, May 19), is one way to encourage this kind of awareness among our students.

What-If Lesson Plan

Instructional Objectives for Students:

- Develop a greater awareness of using what-if thinking skills.

- Understanding that using what-if thinking can prompt deeper thinking into what is.

- Practice PowerPoint and presentation skills.

Duration: Three sixty-minute class periods

Materials:

- Overhead or document camera; computer projector and teacher access to the Internet

- Student copies of Figure 5.9, page 130

- Student access to a computer lab or laptop/tablet cart for one and one-half periods

Common Core English Language Arts Standards

Writing: Produce clear and coherent writing in which the development, organization, and style are appropriate to task, purpose, and audience.

Speaking and Listening: Prepare for and participate effectively in a range of conversations and collaborations with diverse partners, building on others' ideas and expressing their own clearly and persuasively.

Language: Demonstrate command of the conventions of standard English grammar and usage when writing or speaking.

Procedure

First Day:

1. Students walk into class and see "What if you had been born in _____?" written on the overhead or whiteboard. The teacher tells students they should pick a country other than their native one. The teacher gives students thirty seconds to choose a country. Now, the teacher explains, he or she wants students to take five minutes to answer these two questions:

2. ○ How would your life be different from what it is now? Why?

   ○ How would the lives of your friends be different from what they are now? Why?

3. Students write for five minutes while the teacher circulates throughout the classroom.

4. The teacher then asks students to verbally share what they wrote with a partner.

5. The teacher brings the class back together and asks a few students he or she has identified earlier to share their responses.

6. The teacher explains that what happened in the past did not have to happen—it could have happened differently. The history of the United States could have been different—for example, if George Washington had died at Valley Forge. The teacher continues, "You are going to work with a partner, pick one thing that could have happened differently, and explore what consequences that would have for us today."

7. The teacher explains that many attribute the success of people like the creators of Google, Amazon, Wikipedia, the Sims video games, and other innovators like Sean "Diddy" Combs to their ability to regularly ask what-if questions. (The teacher could even create a short read-aloud from a *Wall Street Journal* article on this topic: http://blogs.wsj.com/ideas-mar ket/2011/04/05/the-montessori-mafia.) The teacher says that this is one reason the class is going to do this lesson.

   The teacher places Figure 5.9 on the overhead and explains that students will be using this planning sheet. They can use the textbook, the library, and the Internet to research, and then they will create a five- or six-slide PowerPoint presentation.

   The teacher models completing the planning sheet (he or she can also use Figure 5.9 as just a guide and use a blank planning sheet, Figure 5.10, page 131, and write in the examples). The teacher explains what a "point of divergence" is—it's just another term for the event that happens differently that causes the other things to change.

   The teacher explains that students will work on this project for three days. Today, they will work with partners, decide on their point of divergence, and begin their research. Tomorrow, the class will go to the computer lab or get a laptop/tablet cart and continue their research. After the teacher approves their outlines, they can begin creating their PowerPoint presentation. Then, on the third day, they will have a little more time to prepare and practice their PowerPoint presentation and will show it to the class the second half of the third day.

Here is how one teacher, Carla Federman, explained the assignment to her students:

> You are to identify one specific point in American history for which you are interested in changing the outcome. Once you have identified your point of divergence, you will need to consider both the immediate changes and the long-term impacts that divergence would have on modern society. (Ferlazzo, 2012)

The teacher shows two or three samples of what-if PowerPoint presentations from "The Best Resources For Teaching 'What If?' History Lessons" (www.larryferlazzo.edublogs.org/2012/05/19/the-best-resources-for-teaching-what-if-history-lessons).

8. Students are given the rest of the period to work with partners to decide on their point of divergence and begin research. Each pair of students has to complete only one planning sheet. The teacher circulates, helping students, and collects the sheets unless some students want to work on them at home.

Second Day:

1. The teacher explains that students will either be going to the computer lab or be getting laptops/tablets. They cannot begin working on their PowerPoint presentations until the teacher approves their outlines. The teacher returns the planning sheets.

2. Students research and work on outlines. After receiving teacher approval, they can work on their PowerPoint presentation.

Third Day:

1. The teacher explains that they will have twenty minutes to complete and practice their simple presentations (it could be optional to have students upload their presentations to the Internet; see www.larryferlazzo.edublogs.org/2010/10/26/the-best-sites-where-students-can-upload-powerpoint-presentations-to-the-web). Students go the computer lab or receive laptops/tablets from a cart. The teacher assigns each partner group a number and writes each number on a small sheet of paper, which is then folded and placed in a hat. Students pick numbers to determine who presents first, second, etc. Each presentation should last no longer than four minutes.

2. The teacher explains that during the presentations, each member of the audience will need to write down the name of at least one of the partners presenting and one question to ask. At the end of each presentation, the presenters will choose one member of the audience to ask them a question.

3. At the end of the presentations, audience members turn in their sheets to the teacher. Students are then asked to write responses to three questions (if no class time is left, it can be given as homework):

   o What did you like about the what-if project?

   o How could the project have been better?

   o What did you learn about history?

4. Depending on time, students can discuss in pairs prior to turning in their evaluations to the teacher.

Assessment

- The outline, PowerPoint presentation, and audience questions can be easily assessed.

- If desired, teachers could develop their own rubrics for use with this activity. See "The Best Rubric Sites (And A Beginning Discussion About Their Use)" (www.larryferlazzo.edublogs.org/2010/09/18/the-best-rubric-sites-and-a-beginning-discussion-about-their-use) for multiple free online tools for creating rubrics.

Possible Extensions

Links to more extensive lesson plans developed by Carla Federman and Diana Laufenberg can be found at "The Best Resources For Teaching 'What If?' History Lessons" (www.larryferlazzo.edublogs.org/2012/05/19/the-best-resources-for-teaching-what-if-history-lessons).

Figure 5.9 What-If Planning Sheet Model

Point of Divergence (POD):
George Washington dies at Valley Forge because of the harsh conditions there.
Three New Events as a Result of the POD:

Approximate Date of Event:	Approximate Date of Event:	Approximate Date of Event:
Describe the Event:	Describe the Event:	Describe the Event:
The British win the Revolutionary War.	*Slavery would have been outlawed earlier, and there would not have been a Civil War.*	The United States would *not have gained* territories from Mexico.
Evidence:		Evidence:
The troops were in bad shape at Valley Forge, and many would have deserted if Washington wasn't there to support and inspire them.	Evidence:	*The British had their hands full dealing with big problems in other colonies like India—they probably would not have wanted another war to expand even more in North America.*
	The British outlawed slavery in 1833.	
Source Doc:	Source Doc:	Source Doc:
Textbook/book page or URL address of website where you found the evidence	*Textbook/book page or URL address of website where you found the evidence*	*Textbook/book page or URL address of website where you found the evidence*

■ What would today be like in light of the POD you created? Be specific.

A smaller United States would have probably gotten its independence a lot later, and Great Britain might be a superpower instead of us.

Source: adapted with permission from Diana Laufenberg, n.d., https://sites.google.com/a/scienceleadership.org/what-if-history-project/

Figure 5.10 What-If Planning Sheet

Point of Divergence (POD):		
Approximate Date of Event: Describe the Event: Evidence: Source Doc:	Approximate Date of Event: Describe the Event: Evidence: Source Doc:	Approximate Date of Event: Describe the Event: Evidence: Source Doc:
■ What would today be like in light of the POD you created? Be specific.		

Source: adapted with permission from Diana Laufenberg, n.d., https://sites.google.com/a/scienceleadership.org/what-if-history-project/

Reflection*

Strategically targeted reflection can be a key tool in helping students develop critical and metacognitive thinking capacities. Robert Marzano (2007) calls reflection "the final step in a comprehensive approach to actively processing information" (p. 57). A 2012 analysis of accumulated scientific research found that:

> Mindful introspection can become an effective part of the classroom curriculum, providing students with the skills they need to engage in constructive internal processing and productive reflection. Research indicates that when children are given the time and skills necessary for reflecting, they often become more motivated, less anxious, perform better on tests, and plan more effectively for the future. ("Rest Is Not Idleness," 2012)

Here are a few other easy ways to periodically spend a few minutes—generally, though not always, near the end of class—encouraging "mindful introspection" by students:

Summarize

There is a wealth of research documenting the effectiveness of having students summarize what they have been studying (Wormeli, 2004, p. 2).
Students could respond to prompts like:

♦ What are the two most important things you learned today, and why do you think they are important?

♦ What is the most interesting thing you learned today, and why did you find it so interesting?

♦ What do you know now that you didn't know before today?

♦ What will you tell your parents tonight if they ask what you learned?

♦ Draw something that represents the most important thing you learned today, or that summarizes the day. Please write a short description.

---

*Portions of the following section previously appeared in *The ESL/ELL Teacher's Survival Guide: Ready-to-Use Strategies, Tools, and Activities for Teaching All Levels*, by Larry Ferlazzo and Katie Hull Sypnieski, Jossey-Bass 2012. This material is reproduced with permission of John Wiley & Sons, Inc.

Self-Assess

Marzano (2007, p. 57) recommends students share how well they think they did in class and what they believe they could have done better. Using the metacognitive strategy of reviewing what they did that helped them learn, along with what they did that was not particularly effective, can assist students in developing a greater sense of self-efficacy (Schunk, 2003, p. 4). Here are a few more questions students could answer:

♦ What did you do that helped you the most today to learn the lesson?

♦ What did you do to help yourself understand something when you were not clear?

♦ What, if anything, do you think you need more help in understanding?

♦ What, if anything, are you having difficulty doing?

After students complete the lesson on metacognition found earlier in this chapter, they can review the list of different strategies listed in the student survey and revisit which ones they decided to emphasize.

Assess the Class and the Teacher

Asking students to share their perspectives on class activities and the teacher's style can help on a number of levels. This is best done anonymously to ensure candid responses. Questions could include:

♦ What was your favorite class activity today, and why did you like it?

♦ What was your least favorite class activity today, and why was it your least favorite?

♦ Was the pace of this class too slow, too fast, or just right? Were there particular parts that were too fast or too slow?

Relevance

Some studies have shown that just having students write a few sentences explaining how they could *specifically* apply what they learned to their lives resulted in higher achievement (Hulleman, & Harackiewicz, 2009).

Adapting Bloom's Taxonomy for Reflection

A Taxonomy of Reflection was developed by educator Peter Pappas (2010). In it, he applies the Revised Bloom's Taxonomy to critical reflection. He recommends looking at student self-reflection through this lens:

Creating:	What Should I Do Next?
Evaluating:	How Well Did I Do?
Analyzing:	Do I See Any Patterns in What I Did?
Applying:	Where Could I Use This Again?
Understanding:	What Was Important About It?
Remembering:	What Did I Do?

Some of these questions obviously also connect to the previous reflection ideas. After students become more experienced in self-reflection, and as their English level advances, the teacher might want to start framing the reflection questions in the context of this taxonomy. By doing so, not only may students begin to be more aware of the strategy behind self-reflection, but students will be introduced to (or reminded of) the Revised Bloom's Taxonomy.

Chapter 6

How Can You Get

Students More Interested in Reading and Writing?

Many of my students just don't seem to like to read. And every time I ask them to take out a pencil and piece of paper to write, I'm greeted with a lot of moans and whining. What can I do differently?

This chapter, like most in this book, emphasizes creating the conditions for intrinsic motivation over teaching techniques designed to communicate standards-based content.

However, this focus on strengthening students' appetite for learning can, nevertheless, result in exceptional academic learning of that standards-based content.

It's similar to the perspective held by most effective community organizers—when they approach a problem such as the lack of affordable housing or the need for more neighborhood safety, they first ask themselves, "How can we develop leadership and intrinsic motivation by working on this issue, and then how can that energy be used to get more affordable housing built or more police in the neighborhood?"

They *don't* first ask themselves, "How can we get more affordable housing built or more police in the neighborhood?"

And, nine times out of ten, addressing the first question yields far greater concrete results than trying to tackle the second one. This chapter, and this book, contain ways to apply this same perspective in the classroom to gain similarly positive results.

---

*This chapter has been coauthored by five Sacramento educators: Carolyn Zierenberg, Katie Hull Sypnieski, Dana Dusbiber, Lara Hoekstra, and Larry Ferlazzo.

Let's look at what some research shows to be necessary to create the conditions for intrinsic motivation to flourish, and how that research can be applied specifically to teaching and learning about reading and writing.

Daniel Pink (2011a) has elaborated more on these conditions, building on the Self-Determination Theory (p. 71), developed by Edward Deci and Richard Ryan.

Pink argues that there are three key elements required for the development of intrinsic motivation: autonomy, mastery, and purpose.

Autonomy means "acting with choice" (Pink, 2011a, p. 90). In the area of reading and writing, it could mean having options of books to read, topics to write about, and partners to work with in class. It could also mean teachers having enough of a relationship with students to know their individual hopes and dreams, and then to help students see how lessons are relevant to achieving their goals. It's a recognition by teachers that all of us—including students—are "meant to be players, not pawns. We're meant to be autonomous individuals, not individual automatons" (Pink, 2011a, p. 107).

Mastery of skills that require higher-order thinking is defined by Pink as "the desire to get better and better at something that matters" (Pink, 2011a, p.111), and it is promoted through engagement (coming from the French root word meaning "attract the attention of"), not compliance. Students need to see what reading and writing well can do for them now and in the future. We can support this appetite for mastery in reading and writing by setting up situations where students are likely to be successful (the first chapter discussed how self-efficacy can be a huge motivator); creating opportunities where students can visibly see how much they are improving; and by eliciting from students themselves the multiple situations in their present and future lives where those skills are and will be essential.

Purpose is Pink's final element for developing intrinsic motivation—the desire for some "greater objective ... a cause greater than themselves" (Pink, 2011a, p. 133). The one-sentence project discussed in the first chapter speaks to this point, and we can explore with students how reading and writing well might help them achieve their sentence. Other ideas discussed in this chapter relating to this sense of purpose include reading a book to a younger child, writing articulate letters of thanks and gratitude (see the discussion of gratitude in Chapter 2), and writing letters to the editor or on social media about justice causes they feel strongly about.

This chapter will share immediate actions teachers can take to reinforce Pink's three elements in the areas of reading and writing, including three mini-lessons. These will be divided into separate reading and writing subsections, though, of course, the two are always connected. The setting-the-stage portion of this chapter includes three lesson plans, some which deal equally with reading and writing and others that emphasize one more than the other.

Reading

Free Voluntary Reading or Sustained Silent Reading

Multiple studies have shown that in order for students to motivate themselves to read, they need access to high-interest reading material (Calkins et al., p. 51). According to Calkins, Ehrenworth, and Lehman (2012), "some people suggest the minimum number of books in a classroom library is twenty books per student " (p. 50). In addition to access, students need choice in what they will read (Calkins et al., p. 51). By providing access and choice, students gain a sense of power, and once students feel empowered they are more motivated to read. Strict leveling of books that limit student choice by using predetermined guidelines based on reading level has been found to actually discourage reading motivation (British Columbia Teacher Librarians' Association, 2009). Instead, students can be encouraged to choose "just right" books that are engaging and accessible. Though classroom book access is easier for students, the school library is obviously another source for books.

Of course, once students identify the books they want to read, there is the question of how best to support them reading in the classroom. Silent sustained reading, also sometimes called free voluntary reading, is designed to have students read for pleasure with minimal paperwork accountability, and there is substantial research showing that it enhances student motivation to read and increases academic gains (Ferlazzo, 2011; Garan & DeVoogd, 2008).

Having students spend fifteen minutes at the beginning of each or most class periods, and having them read books of their choice for thirty minutes each evening, is one way to encourage reading for pleasure. Though some teachers feel that it is important for them to model reading a book during this classroom reading time, studies have suggested that, instead, students can benefit most by teachers circulating and providing individual feedback (having short conversations about the book, discussing the use of reading strategies, etc.) ("Best Uses of Independent Reading Time," 2011).

Ed Tech
The Joy of Reading

Many schools, classes, individuals, and groups have developed engaging videos celebrating the joy of reading. You can find a collection of them at "The Best Fun Videos About Books & Reading" (www.larryferlazzo.edublogs.org/2012/03/26/the-best-fun-videos-about-books-reading). Teachers can show them to their class and consider if they, too, want to create one.

Reading and the Brain

There has been extensive research on the physical changes reading can produce in the brain, ranging from a possible connection between cortical thickness and extensive pleasure reading (Goldman & Manis, 2012) to descriptions of the impact the relatively recent invention of reading has on the brain (Wolf & Barzillai, 2009). The following mini-lesson reviews this research. This mini-lesson will help students see the direct impact reading has on altering their brains.

Mini-Lesson: Reading and the Brain

1. Students enter the room with this question on the whiteboard or overhead: "How old is humanity?" The teacher explains he or she wants students to take thirty seconds and think silently about the answer.

   After thirty seconds, the teacher asks certain students to share their numbers (the answer is between 2.4 and 7 million years old) (Holladay, 2004).

   Next, the teacher asks students to take out a sheet of paper and make a list of things they believe early humans could do, like walking or hunting. The teacher asks students to keep their answers clean (in a humorous tone). After a minute, he or she tells students to share their answers with a partner. Next, the teacher calls on students and makes a list on the overhead or whiteboard, in a T-chart, with how old humanity is as the title on one side and a list of what early humans were able to do underneath. The other side should remain blank.

   Then the teacher writes "reading" in the other column—across from the basic abilities students listed. The teacher asks students to take thirty seconds to think about when they think humans began to read. He or she then asks students what they thought, and ultimately informs them that reading was invented only 5,500 years ago (and writes that as the title of the second column). The teacher emphasizes that the brain is not born being able to read—we change our brains in order to read.

2. The teacher places Figure 6.1 on the overhead and asks students to read silently as he or she reads it aloud. He or she then passes out copies of the read-aloud.

3. The teacher then shows the two short videos of Maryanne Wolf speaking about reading and the brain. They can be found at www. larryferlazzo.edublogs.org/2011/11/26/the-best-resources-for-showing-students-that-they-make-their-brain-stronger-by-learning.

Figure 6.1 Reading and Your Brain Read-Aloud

A 2012 study found that people who read more for pleasure had greater cortical thickness (cortical refers to the cortex, a portion of the brain) than those who read less or not at all: "The pattern of correlations indicated that individuals with higher print exposure had better reading skills and thicker cortices.... This suggests that some of the variation in cortical thickness in adults might be attributable to reading experience" (Goldman & Manis, 2012).

Reading is a new function of our brains that humans invented 5,500 years ago. It is in our genes to see, hear, taste, move, etc., but our brains reprogram themselves to read. The pathways change in our brains as we begin to learn to go beyond decoding (just knowing how to say the words) to understanding their meaning and connecting our own prior knowledge and experiences to them.

Researcher and author Maryanne Wolf writes that using reading strategies like asking questions and making connections to background knowledge will eventually, with practice, take shorter periods of time: "A few hundred milliseconds to be exact.... By the time the expert reader has comprehended a text at a deep level, all four lobes and both hemispheres of the brain have contributed significantly to this extraordinary act.... What we read and how deeply we read shape both the brain and the thinker" (Wolf & Barzillai, 2009).

4. The teacher explains that students need to write a short paragraph using the ABC format (Answer the question; Back it up with a quote or other evidence; make a Connection to an experience or another text). They have to answer this question:

"What impact does reading have on the brain?"

The teacher asks students to imagine their audience is someone who does not believe it has any impact at all. He or she says that they will have ten minutes to write.

5. After ten minutes, the teacher can either collect the papers or, if there is time, first have students verbally share what they wrote with a partner.

Read a Book to a Younger Child

Having students read a book to a younger child can achieve two results—helping students develop a sense of purpose (discussed earlier in this chapter) connected to reading *and* strengthening prosody—rhythm, intonation, and fluency. If desired, Figure 6.2, page 140, can be completed by the students and turned in to the teacher as extra credit.

Figure 6.2 Read a Children's Book

Student name: _____

1. What is the name of the child you read the book to?

2. What is the child's relationship to you?

3. What is the title of the book you read?

4. Why did you pick that book?

5. Did the child enjoy having you read the book to him or her? How could you tell?

6. How did you feel about reading the book to him or her? Why?

Source: From *The ESL/ELL Teacher's Survival Guide: Ready-to-Use Strategies, Tools, and Activities for Teaching All Levels,* by Larry Ferlazzo and Katie Hull Sypnieski, 2012, Jossey Bass. This material is reproduced with permission of John Wiley & Sons, Inc.

Book Talks

It's not unusual for adults to talk about books they're reading, so why not have students do the same? Teachers can create a simple form that would take students five minutes to complete, asking questions like: "What is the title of the book? What is the book about? Who is your favorite character and why? What is your favorite passage, and why do you like it?" The questions could periodically change. Then, in small groups, students can show their books in small groups, verbally share what they wrote, and ask questions of one another.

Ed Tech
Writing Book Reviews for Authentic Audiences and Creating Video Book Reviews

The motivating value of writing for an authentic audience beyond the teacher was discussed in earlier chapters. This can be applied to book reviews, too. There are many free sites where students can post their reviews, and a list can be found at "The Best Places Where Students can Post Book Reviews For Authentic Audiences" (www.larryferlazzo.edublogs.org/2012/08/11/the-best-places-where-students-can-post-book-reviews-for-authentic-audiences).

Students can also create video book reviews and post them online at a class blog. They can be a simple reading of what students wrote on the form the teacher created, or elaborate productions with props and costumes. Details and examples can be found at "My Best Posts On Books: Why They're Important & How To Help Students Select, Read, Write, & Discuss Them" (www.larryferlazzo.edublogs.org/2010/05/30/my-best-posts-on-books-why-theyre-important-how-to-help-students-select-read-write-discuss-them).

Reading and Getting a Job

A 2011 Oxford University study found that reading for pleasure was the only activity done by teenagers in their free time that had a direct connection to helping them get a better job in the future ("Reading at 16," 2011). This simple mini-lesson uses the results of that study.

Mini–Lesson: Reading and Getting a Job

1. The teacher asks students to think for a minute and make a list of what they do in their free time. Students are given two minutes to write.

2. The teacher then asks students to share what they wrote and makes a list on the whiteboard or overhead. It doesn't have to be an exhaustive list—just a sample.

3. The teacher then explains that they are going to read two very short articles about a study that reviews what teenagers do in their free time and what activities can help them get better jobs in the future. He or she tells students that the articles are very similar, but each has information the other does not. Students are to work in pairs and take turns reading paragraphs to one another. After they are done reading, they are to:

   ♦ Write a one-sentence summary of what they learned.

   ♦ Pick two passages (one or two sentences each) from the articles that they think are most interesting or important and write why they think so: (1) www.telegraph.co.uk/foodanddrink/8435031/Reading-as-teenager-gets-you-a-better-job.html; (2) www.ox.ac.uk/media/news_stories/2011/110804.html

   Students are given fifteen minutes to read and write.

4. The teacher brings students back together and asks a few individual students to share. The teacher then either just collects the papers or, if there is time available, first asks students to pick one of the quotations and put it on an illustrated poster that can then be hung on the classroom walls.

Writing

Publishing on a Small Scale

One way to encourage students to see themselves as writers is to publish student work. This can often be a time consuming and expensive task. One way to avoid this is to publish on a smaller scale; Kelly Gallagher (2006), author of *Teaching Adolescent Writers,* refers to this idea as "Golden Lines." After students have written, formally or informally, have them select their best lines. They may choose a phrase or a whole sentence, but no more than two or three sentences. Teachers can have students highlight the sentence or write it on a Post-it note. Students can remain anonymous or take ownership. Teachers could post the notes on the wall or compile them into one document. Typing them up and giving them to the class allows students to see their work published alongside their classmates'. Students usually pore over the document looking for their own lines and then read their classmates' work. Various options for publishing student work on the Web have also been previously mentioned.

Writing Frames

Sometimes when students are faced with a blank page, they freeze. Giving students structures for writing can be motivational. However, when taken too far, or when taught as the *only* way to write, writing formulas can be detrimental to students' growth as writers. When used correctly, formulas and strategies can help students to find their voices and motivate them to write. If they believe they can be successful, then they are more motivated to try. Instead of staring at a blank page, they have something to start with.

There are a variety of acronyms for structured paragraph writing to help students: ABC, PQC, PEA, SSE, PEE. We have found ABC and PQC to be effective in helping students to start their writings. Using the ABC format, students Answer the question; Back it up with a quote or other evidence; make a Connection to an experience or another text (or make a Comment). If the teacher is working on quote integration or using quotations from text as evidence, then PQC is a good start: Make a Point; Quote from the text supporting your point; make a Comment or a connection to your personal experience, another text, or some other knowledge. Other variations are PEA (make a Point, provide Evidence, Analyze the evidence by connecting it to the point), SSE (Summarize the issue, take a Stance, provide Evidence to support the stance), and PEE (make a Point, provide Evidence, Explain how the evidence proves the point). All of these formats represent some variation of students making a point, providing evidence, and analyzing this evidence.

Sometimes reluctant writers may also need sentence frames, or paragraph frames, to help them express their ideas in writing. Figure 6.3, page 144, contains an ABC paragraph frame and two examples.

Responding to Writing Prompts

Many of our students feel anxiety when given a writing prompt, especially in a testing situation when they must produce writing on demand in a certain amount of time. We have found one way to ease this anxiety and to help students feel more confident when faced with writing prompts is to let them practice carefully reading and "attacking" a prompt. We model this process first and then have students practice multiple times throughout the year.

The first step we model is to read the prompt carefully and circle or underline any key words or phrases, especially words telling us to do something and/or words that are repeated. Then we have students number the specific tasks or questions they need to respond to (i.e., what they must do first, second, etc.). We may also have them draw a box for each number that they can use as a graphic organizer to list ideas and words. For more complicated prompts, we may have students work in pairs to rewrite

Figure 6.3   ABC Paragraph Frames and Examples

Question

Why would people describe Tupac Shakur as a thug angel?

Frame

People describe Tupac Shakur as a thug angel because _____
_____. One reason people say he was a thug is
_____. Some other reasons
are _____. Despite this, he
was also considered an angel because _____.
He also _____.
Like many others, Tupac had two sides; _____
_____.

Examples

People describe Tupac Shakur as a thug angel because he had both good and
bad qualities. One reason people say he was a thug is he had several encoun-
ters with the police. Some other reasons are he was arrested, served time in
prison for sexual assault, smoked pot, and owned a lot of guns. Despite this,
he was also considered an angel because he wasn't always bad. When he was
a student in Baltimore, he set up a lot of clubs to stop violence, and he even
wrote his first rap condemning gun violence. He also continued to help people
throughout his rap career. Many artists, like Mac Mall, credit Tupac with giving
them a break in the rap industry. Like many others, Tupac had two sides; he
did some bad things, but he also did some good things, and that is why some
people describe him as a thug angel.

Question

Why do people join gangs?

Example

People join gangs for various reasons. Most people think that they've joined
gangs because they're uneducated and do nothing but drugs, steal, and kill. I
personally think that people join gangs to gain the respect of others surrounding
them. To prove to themselves and others that they are strong and capable to do
anything on their own. In exemplar number eighteen it says, "They join gangs
to protect themselves, to be in control of their own lives." This is so true! I have
family members who are gang affiliated. They don't hurt people, they just want
to protect themselves and also their family.

the key tasks in their own words. We also encourage students to reflect on which strategies help them the most when attacking a prompt and why, as well as inviting them to think of new strategies to try.

Inductive Learning

Chapter 5 on higher-order thinking skills discussed inductive learning, and Chapter 4 on classroom management contained a lesson on stress where an inductive data set was used as scaffolding for students to write an essay.

Briefly, inductive teaching can be an instructional strategy of presenting students with numerous examples of information on a broader topic (called a data set)—let's say Jamaica—and then having students categorize the information.

In terms of writing, this categorization activity is easily transferable to writing—the categories can then be converted into paragraphs, and students can easily cite their sources. It's a very accessible process that students can use in writing whatever they need to in any class—even when they don't actually have a formal data set. When they're reading a textbook, for example, they just need to convert whatever notes they've taken into categories.

Feelings of self-efficacy are important for the development of intrinsic motivation. Easily transferable tools, like this inductive method, can help students feel confident in writing. The more confident they feel, the more they will *want* to do it.

Setting the Stage

Our World of Text

Students often do not see the relevance that reading and writing have in their lives. Assisting students to see themselves as readers and writers in the world at large will help them to approach academic reading and writing with renewed interest and a more positive attitude. Moreover, when students are aware of the benefits of reading and writing certain texts well, they will be more motivated to improve as readers and writers.

This lesson plan begins with validating students as readers and writers; it allows them to see that there are different ways to read and write and that the teacher values their knowledge and experience. After students' prior knowledge is validated, students are invited to figure out why reading and writing well is important to them, and what they will get out of being better readers and writers. This lesson plan helps students to see why it is in their own self-interest to improve as readers and writers.

The idea of using a PowerPoint representation of different texts to validate students' prior knowledge as readers comes from Belinda Foster, a teacher in the Twin Rivers Unified School District in Sacramento, and a teacher consultant for the Area 3 Writing Project out of the University of California, Davis.

Becoming an Expert Through Deliberate Practice

This lesson introduces the concept of deliberate practice and provides text models for students that show what this practice looks like in real life. Anders Ericsson, who first developed this concept, defined it this way: "In most domains of expertise, individuals begin in their childhood a regimen of effortful activities (deliberate practice) designed to optimize improvement. Individual differences, even among elite performers, are closely related to assessed amounts of deliberate practice" (Ericsson, Krampe & Tesch-Römer, 1993, p. 1). Ericsson was clear that one's ability to become an expert had more to do with focused practice than innate talent. He was also clear that this kind of practice ought to be sustained over the course of 10 years. We point this out to the students when discussing their own journeys toward literacy expertise.

Through their own understanding of deliberate practice theory, students will have the opportunity to think of their own literacy—their intelligence as readers and writers—as a valued skill set at which they can become experts. When we allow them to reflect on how much practice they have already completed toward individual literacy mastery, they can then set achievable goals and work toward them, with our help, during the school year. This lesson can be a follow-up lesson to the "Our World of Text" lesson.

Authentic Audience

This lesson plan is designed so that students have an authentic audience for their writing. We have found that students will engage in writing activities when they feel a sense of purpose beyond just the letter grade in a grade book. This activity helps students voice their opinions about a topic that directly influences them in a format that is approachable. Utilizing writing prompts from Kelly Young of Pebble Creek Labs to set the stage for brainstorming, students feel a sense of authorship as their initial "quickwrites" become the "expert opinion" cited in their longer formal piece. This lesson plans uses the text analysis acronym TAPS (topic, audience, purpose, speaker) introduced to us by Belinda Foster. Student samples of the two different letters to teachers are also included at the end of this lesson plan. Those can be one of the final products coming out of the lesson.

"Our World of Text" Lesson Plan

Instructional Objectives for Students:

- Learn why writing and reading matter in their own lives.

- Analyze various texts and determine topic, audience, and purpose.

- Demonstrate an understanding of topic, audience, and purpose.

Duration: Two sixty-minute class periods

Materials:

- A piece of unusual text, hung on the wall or board

- Document camera or overhead projector, computer, connection to Internet

- Teacher-created PowerPoint presentation, containing a range of texts

- Student copies of Figure 6.4, page 152

- Teacher-created T-chart poster "Why We Read and Write"

- Teacher-created T-chart poster "What We Read and Write"

- Copies for each student of "Daily Writing Scenarios" sheet, similar to the one pictured in Figure 6.5, page 152

- Copy of "Daily Reading Scenarios" sheet, similar to the one pictured in Figure 6.6, page 154, cut into strips, one strip per student

- Sticky notes or paper for students to brainstorm ideas

- Paragraph frame for assessment (Figure 6.7, page 154)

Common Core English Language Arts Standards

Reading:

- Determine a central idea of a text.

- Determine an author's point of view or purpose in a text.

Writing: Produce clear and coherent writing in which the development, organization, and style are appropriate to task, purpose, and audience.

Speaking and Listening:

- Prepare for and participate effectively in a range of conversations and collaborations with diverse partners, building on others' ideas and expressing their own clearly and persuasively.

- Adapt speech to a variety of contexts and communicative tasks, demonstrating command of formal English when indicated or appropriate.

Language:

- Demonstrate command of the conventions of standard English grammar and usage when writing or speaking.

- Demonstrate command of the conventions of standard English capitalization, punctuation, and spelling when writing.

Procedure

First Day:

1. The teacher posts an unusual piece of text (computer code, text message, diagram of a football play, something written in a different language, etc.) on the board. The teacher does not address the text and continues with the lesson.

2. The teacher tells students they will be exploring why people, including students, read and write. He or she tells them that they are going to be watching a PowerPoint presentation featuring a variety of texts. The teacher defines the following terms: topic (what the piece is about), audience (who was intended to read the piece), and purpose (why the author wrote this piece). The teacher tells students that as they watch they should be thinking about the topic, audience, and purpose of the text.

3. The teacher explains that everyone is proficient at reading and writing, depending upon the text. The teacher models with an "unusual" piece of text that he or she is familiar with, like a map (the meaning of symbols, boundaries, etc.), and the teacher reads the text to the class.

4. The teacher shows the PowerPoint presentation (samples can be found at "Reading & Writing PowerPoints," www.larryferlazzo.edublogs.org/wiki/reading-writing-powerpoints). It should have a variety of texts; for example, a football play, musical score, computer code, texting language, advertisement, blog, etc. Knowing the students in the class can help to determine what texts the teacher shows. For each slide the class should discuss the topic, audience, and purpose. The teacher should also ask the class who can read certain texts, making sure to elicit responses from different students with different strengths. For example, there may be a student in the class

who can "read" the lines of a basketball court and tell the class what each line means. Steps 1–4 should take twenty to thirty minutes. The teacher can point out that students are reading, analyzing and finding meaning in different types of text all the time—they just have to apply those same skills to words on a page.

5. After showing the PowerPoint presentation, the teacher has students list other texts they can, and do, read and write. Students share in pairs and then with the class. As the students share with the class, the teacher records the ideas on a poster labeled "What We Read and Write."

6. Teacher passes out Figure 6.4. Before having students fill out the sheet, he or she models, writing something like "to get information about a topic." He or she asks students to fill out the box labeled "Why People Read." Students should write and then share what they wrote with partners, and the teacher can ask a few to share with the class. The teacher continues this process until all four squares are completed. As students share with the class, the teacher records comments on a T-chart poster labeled "Why We Read and Write."

7. To end the class, the teacher returns to the unusual text posted in the room and asks students to think about its topic, audience, and purpose. The teacher passes out paper or Post-it notes and asks students to write why they believe someone wrote this text or why someone would read it. The teacher collects the work as students exit the classroom. Steps 5–7 should take about twenty-five minutes.

Second Day:

1. The teacher has the "Why We Read and Write" poster from the previous day displayed on the board, as well as the poster "What We Read and Write" listing the things students read and write, also created the previous day.

2. The teacher asks students to review the list of what they read and write. The teacher then asks the students to think about the following question: "What's in it for you if you do these things well?" The teacher picks something from the student-generated list and models for the students, reflecting on the topic, audience, and purpose and then explaining how he or she will benefit by doing it well. For example, the teacher might say, "A text to a friend about where to meet. If I am unclear, then we may miss each other, and maybe we have a fight or are angry with each other. If I do this well, then the other person will know where to meet, and there won't be any problems."

3. The teacher then picks another text from the list and asks, "What is the topic? Audience? Purpose?" The teacher then asks, "What do you get out of it if you write this well?" Before calling on students, the teacher has them turn to the person next to them and share their answers. He or she calls on

a few students to share ideas with the class. The teacher then comes up with a couple of other scenarios. The teacher says something like, "You're asked to write a eulogy for your grandmother's funeral. What do you get out of it if you do it well?" Or, "Your family is unhappy with a dinner they had at a restaurant. You want to write a letter of complaint. How could you benefit if you write this letter well?" Steps 1–3 should take about fifteen minutes.

4. The teacher then divides the class into pairs and displays Figure 6.5. The teacher asks students to think about these types of writing and to choose one they think they may have to write some time after high school (the teacher, of course, can add other writing scenarios he/she thinks are appropriate to the class). The teacher then assigns each pair another scenario, so that all scenarios are represented. Students should brainstorm the topic, audience, and purpose of each of the writings, as well as how students can benefit from writing these texts well. The teacher can ask a few to share with the class, making sure each of the scenarios is covered. Another option is to turn this activity into a game. Students could be divided into small groups and given handheld whiteboards if available. Instead of displaying Figure 6.5, the teacher could read each individual scenario and ask students to write down the topic, audience, and purpose of each one, as well as student benefits. The best answers could receive "points" to determine the winner or winners. This should take about twenty minutes.

5. The teacher displays Figure 6.6. Students are going to be asked to write scenarios similar to the list of daily writing scenarios (Figure 6.5). The teacher models recipe one for the class, saying something like, "A recipe for my mom's macaroni and cheese. The topic is how to make macaroni and cheese. The audience is someone who wants to make it. The purpose is to make sure that someone makes it correctly so that it tastes good. I need to make sure I read this and understand it because my family is counting on me to prepare this the right way. If I understand it and can follow it, then everyone is going to enjoy the food and they won't get sick. I want to honor my mother, so I'm going to work hard and learn the abbreviations so the family will be happy."

6. The teacher passes out one strip of paper (containing one example of a text people are likely to read) to each student. Students should brainstorm a scenario for this type of reading. After coming up with a scenario, they need to write down the topic, audience, purpose, and what someone would get out of doing it well. Students could create a poster with this information. Students then share their scenarios through "speed dating." This is a quick way for students to share their work with several different partners. They simply line up in two rows facing each other, and the teacher designates one row to be the "movers" while the other row will not move.

Each student shares his or her work with the person facing him or her. After enough time has gone by for both partners to share, the teacher calls out "Switch!" and the movers step to the right so they are now facing new partners. Repeating this process allows students to share with several different partners. Students can share in numerous ways (reading something they've written, explaining one part of their work, etc.) Steps 5–6 should take about twenty-five minutes.

Assessment

- The teacher asks students to reflect on the writings and conversations from yesterday and today and to think about these questions: What is an important text that you need to be able to read and why? What is an important text that you need to write well and why?

- Students write two paragraphs answering these questions. Students should use the ABC format to respond. The teacher can also provide the paragraph frame in Figure 6.7. The teacher collects the paragraphs.

Possible Extensions

- Students could make posters about genres or topics they are interested in reading about outside of class.

- Students could make posters outlining what they want to accomplish as readers and writers for the year.

- Students could research a career they are interested in and the types of reading and writing required for that career.

- Students can set reading goals for the semester (see *Helping Students Motivate Themselves,* pp. 7–12 for reading goals). Teachers could also create their own writing goal sheets for students to complete.

Figure 6.4 Why We Read and Write

Why People Read	Why I Read
Why People Write	**Why I Write**

Figure 6.5 Daily Writing Scenarios

Listed below are a variety of texts that people are likely to be asked to write.

Memos

- Your boss asks you to write a memo to be distributed to all other employees detailing the company's new rules regarding computer use.

Reports

- You are out with friends, and you are the passenger in a car. There is an auto accident and it is unclear who was at fault, your friend or the other driver. The police ask you to write a report.

Correspondence

- You have just interviewed at a job you really want, so you send an e-mail thanking the interviewer.

Figure 6.5   Daily Writing Scenarios (*continued*)

- You saved your money and bought the car of your dreams. While still under warranty, it continuously breaks down and you need to write a letter to the dealership to have the issue fixed or to ask for a new car.
- Your wallet slipped out of your pocket on the bus. Someone found your wallet, located you using your driver's license, and dropped the wallet off at your house. All of your money and belongings are still in it. You write the person a letter saying thank you.
- You have been working a lot lately and suddenly realize you missed your friend's birthday. You write him or her an apology text.

Lists

- You are leaving on a trip, and a friend is watching your place. Your friend has asked you to leave a list detailing how to take care of your house and animals.
- Your employer has asked you to compile a list detailing what materials you and your coworkers need for a project.

Directions

- You will be out of the office and another employee will have to take over some of your job duties. You need to provide directions on how to complete your duties.
- Family members from out of town are staying with you. While you are at work they will be touring the city and have asked you for directions on how to get to some of your favorite places.

Notes

- You are having lunch with your boss and come up with a good idea for work. Your boss asks you to take notes so you both can remember the important details.
- You have been stressed and not paying attention to your partner. You are leaving on a business trip early in the morning, so you write a note telling him or her how much he or she means to you, and you promise to try to be less stressed about work after the trip.

Action Plans

- You have discovered a way to help your workplace run more efficiently. Your boss asks you to write an action plan on how to accomplish this.

Eulogy/Toast

- Your grandmother has died, and your mother asks you to write and deliver the eulogy at her funeral.
- Your best friend gets married and asks you to write and deliver the toast at his or her wedding.

Figure 6.6   Daily Reading Scenarios

Listed below are a variety of texts that people are likely to read.

Recipes

- Your family reunion is coming up. This is the first one you have attended since your mother passed away. Your family has asked you to make your mother's macaroni and cheese, a favorite among all family members. Your mom's handwritten recipe is full of abbreviations and unfamiliar cooking terms.

Memos	**Action plans**
Reports	**Newspaper articles**
Lists	**Blogs**
Directions	**Textbook**
Handbooks	**Training manuals**
Notes	**Instructions**

Correspondence (letters, texts, e-mails, etc.)

Journals and articles relevant to a trade or career

Figure 6.7   Sample ABC Paragraph Frame

Question: What is an important text that you need to be able to read and why?

I feel that it is important for me to read _____ well. If I read _____ and understand it, I will benefit because _____ _____. I want to be able to do this because _____.

Question: What is an important text that you need to write well and why?

It is important for me to be able to write _____ well. If I am able to successfully write _____, I will benefit because _____. This is important to me because _____.

Becoming an Expert Through Deliberate Practice Lesson Plan

Instructional Objectives for Students:

- Learn how deliberate practice leads to mastery of a skill.

- Understand the theory of deliberate practice so that they can apply its keys to their own future reading and writing practice and goals.

- Make individual learning goals, incorporating deliberate practice.

Duration: Two and a half sixty-minute class periods

Materials:

- Document camera or overhead projector

- Copy of teacher questions to be posted on document camera or overhead

- Student copies of Figure 6.8, page 159

- Teacher/student copies of three read-alouds (Figures 6.9, 6.10, and 6.11 [pages 160–161])

- Copies of Figures 6.12, page 161, and 6.13, page 162

- Computer and projection screen and access to the Internet

- Poster paper or chart paper

- Large sticky notes or colored construction paper for writing

- Student journals or paper for writing

Common Core English Language Arts Standards

Reading:

- Determine the central ideas or themes of a text and analyze their development; summarize the key supporting details and ideas.

- Interpret words and phrases as they are used in a text, including determining technical, connotative, and figurative meanings, and analyze how specific word choices shape meaning or tone.

Writing: Produce clear and coherent writing in which the development, organization, and style are appropriate to task, purpose, and audience.

Speaking and Listening: Prepare for and participate effectively in a range of conversations and collaborations with diverse partners, building on others' ideas and expressing their own clearly and persuasively.

Procedure

First Day:

1. The teacher poses the following question, posted on the whiteboard or doc cam: "If you could become an expert at anything, knowing that it would take a lot of practice, what would you choose?"

2. Students write their responses on paper or in their journals and then share with a partner. The teacher provides five to ten minutes for quiet writing and then a few minutes for partner sharing.

3. The teacher asks for student volunteers to share responses with the class.

4. The teacher then asks, "Can you guess how many hours someone might need to practice to be an expert, to master something?"

5. Students share number guesses with partners, and the teacher calls on partner groups to share with class. The teacher writes these numbers on the whiteboard or doc cam.

6. The teacher then poses this question, also written on the board or on paper for the doc cam: "Now, think about something that you do, almost every day, that might put you close to the expert category … this could be something you do in school, at home, or anyplace else. Write down your response."

7. Students write in journals, and the teacher allows for partner or whole-class sharing and discussion. The writing and sharing should take about 10 minutes.

8. At this point, the teacher might comment on a skill he or she possesses that would help students to make connections. The teacher might say, "I am close to being at expert at _____ because I started practicing as a child and still put time into this pursuit today." The teacher might also speak about his or her own literacy journey—the practice and rewards of being a good writer and reader.

9. Introduce the following statement to students by posting it on the whiteboard or doc cam: "Experts agree that 10,000 hours is the number that most people will dedicate to becoming an "expert" at any given skill. It takes about 10 years to get to the 10,000 hour mark" (Ericsson, 1993).

10. The teacher introduces the YouTube video at www.youtube.com/watch?v=Kq2n1Jlx5PO. It includes footage from an Anderson Cooper interview with Malcolm Gladwell. The teacher allows ten minutes for watching the video and student questions.

11. The teacher tells students that the class is going to spend some time thinking about how these deliberate-practice facts apply to their own reading and writing development. The teacher might say something like, "We already have a head start on reading and writing practice, and the next part of the lesson will focus on that practice. You can use this information to get better at anything, but we're going to focus on reading and writing."

Second Day:

1. The teacher asks students to spend a few moments writing in their journals, remembering what they learned about deliberate practice and jotting down any questions they have about the theory or how it works to help people get good at something.

2. The teacher presents Figure 6.8 to students by posting it on the camera and providing each student with a copy. Students should be instructed to keep this paper in their folders or attach it to their journals. The teacher reads the figures to students and notes with them that they have already put in a significant number of hours toward their own literacy expertise. (Note: The numbers provided are estimations based on the number of hours *most* students dedicate to literacy in their elementary and middle school years. The numbers will vary from district to district and within schools.)

3. The teacher asks students to work with a partner to add up the numbers and then determine approximately how many hours they would need in college to get to the 10,000-hour mark. Post this figure on the whiteboard and make a big deal about how many hours they have already dedicated to this practice.

4. The teacher says, "Now we are going to read some passages that will give us a better idea of what deliberate practice is and how people use it to become experts."

5. The teacher distributes Figure 6.9 to the class. The teacher places the passage under the camera and reads the passage aloud to the class, as students follow along silently. The teacher provides students with large sticky notes and instructs them to address the prompt at the bottom of the read-aloud. Students write for five to seven minutes. Students may share with a partner and post responses on a class poster called "Notes on Deliberate Practice."

6. The teacher distributes and reads Figure 6.10 to the class. While reading, the teacher briefly defines any vocabulary students might need help with (such as the word *earnest*). Students again answer the question at the bottom of the prompt. This time the teacher instructs students to write in their journals or on paper. The teacher opens up discussion to the whole class. Writing should take ten minutes, with the discussion taking several more.

7. The teacher distributes Figure 6.11. Students read this passage independently. With a partner, students will write their own definitions of deliberate practice. Provide either large sticky notes or colored construction paper cut into large (5 x 5) squares. Student groups will write their definitions on the paper provided, share aloud with the class, and post them on the class poster. The teachers allows ten to fifteen minutes for the writing, sharing, and posting of definitions.

8. The teacher tells students that now the class is going to look at some of the important features of deliberate practice and think about setting goals to improve their practice toward reading and writing expertise.

Third Day:

1. The teacher invites students to look at their writings from the previous day and revisits the class poster "Notes on Deliberate Practice." Students share with a partner what they learned from the lesson about deliberate practice for five minutes or so.

2. The teacher informs students that they are going to set some goals that will help them get closer to the expert range.

3. The teacher distributes Figure 6.12. This guide sheet should become a reference for teacher and learners to revisit throughout the year. Each of the "keys" correlates with effective and ongoing instruction and student practice in a literacy-based classroom setting. For this lesson, the teacher will select two or three items from the guide on which to focus for immediate goal setting related to in-class or independent reading. The teacher reads aloud each key and sample goal.

4. Students will now make their own goals related to their reading. Provide students with the goal-setting sheet (Figure 6.13) and remind them that the five keys sheet (Figure 6.12) includes models for student-composed goals. Students should set two goals for the first quarter (this should take fifteen minutes). The teacher collects the goals and informs students that he or she will make a copy of their goals in order to know what they will be working toward.

Assessment

- The teacher can review and assess student responses to read-aloud prompts and student-written goals.

- If desired, teachers could develop their own rubrics for use with this activity. See "The Best Rubric Sites (And A Beginning Discussion About Their Use)" (www.larryferlazzo.edublogs.org/2010/09/18/the-best-rubric-sites-and-a-beginning-discussion-about-their-use) for multiple free online tools for creating rubrics.

Possible Extensions

The teacher can show students the infographic on deliberate practice at www.larryferlazzo.edublogs.org/2012/07/21/the-best-resources-for-learning-about-the-10000-hour-rule-deliberative-practice, and students can create their own infographic on the topic—either with markers and paper or online (see Ed Tech box).

Ed Tech
Creating Infographics

Since studies have shown we are more likely to remember information presented visually (www.bbc.co.uk/news/business-17682294), showing and creating infographics in the classroom can be a useful instructional strategy. There are many simple and free tools that can let students create an infographic, and a list of them can be found at "The Best Resources For Creating Infographics" (www.larryferlazzo.edublogs.org/2011/01/11/the-best-resources-for-creating-infographics).

Figure 6.8   Literacy Mastery

Literacy Mastery

- In kindergarten through grade 5, you spent approximately 2,160 hours practicing literacy (about two hours each day).

- In grades 6–8, your hours were approximately 1,620 (three hours each day).

- In high school, you will practice literacy two to three hours each day, to get to approximately 2,160 hours.

- By the time you graduate from college, you will be an expert reader and writer!

Figure 6.9 Read-Aloud #1

Bobby Meacham was a minor-league manager who saw Alex Rodriguez when he first began playing professional baseball: "'This guy goes about his business not like he wants to get to the big leagues, but like he wants to be the best,' Meacham said. 'He knows he's going to be good, but he wants to be great. There was just a **method** to it'" (Kepner, 2008, para. 3–4).

Meacham went on to describe how Rodriguez would have balls hit to him in different ways and how he was methodical in trying to hit to different places when he was at batting practice: "'At 18 or 19 years old, he already had a **plan**,' Meacham said. 'It was pretty awesome to watch'" (para. 6).

Writing Prompt: Meacham speaks about Rodriguez's approach to getting great at baseball. What do you think he means when he talks about Rodriguez's method and plan?

Figure 6.10 Read-Aloud #2

Benjamin Bloom, an eminent educational researcher, studied 120 outstanding achievers. They were concert pianists, sculptors, Olympic swimmers, world-class tennis players, mathematicians, and research neurologists. Most were not that remarkable as children and didn't show clear talent before their training began in **earnest**. Even by early adolescence, you usually couldn't predict their future accomplishment from their current ability. Only their continued motivation and commitment, along with their network of support, took them to the top. Bloom concludes, "After forty years of intensive research on school learning in the United States as well as abroad, my major conclusion is: What any person in the world can learn, almost all persons can learn, if provided with the appropriate prior and current conditions of learning." He's not counting the 2 to 3 percent of children who have severe impairments, and he's not counting the top 1 to 2 percent of children at the other extreme…. He is counting everybody else. (Dweck, 2006, pp. 65–66)

Writing Prompt: Bloom believes that any person can learn anything, when the proper conditions for learning are met. Write about what you believe are good conditions for learning.

Figure 6.11   Read-Aloud #3

> "Deliberate practice requires careful reflection on what worked and what didn't work. A budding concert pianist may practice a particularly troublesome passage listening for places where his fingers do not flow smoothly…. This kind of practice demands time for reflection and intense concentration, so intense that it is difficult to sustain for longer than 3 hours per day" (Mahajan, 2011).
>
> **Writing Prompt:** Write your own one- or two-sentence definition of deliberate practice, and post your definition on the paper strips provided.

Figure 6.12   Five Keys to Getting Great Through Deliberate Practice

1. **Do the hardest work first.** We all move toward pleasure and away from pain. Most great performers practice in the mornings. We schedule our reading time here in the classroom at the beginning of the period.

   Sample Goal: "I will read for the first twenty minutes of class each day, before I do anything else at school."

2. **Practice intensely.** Practice without interruption for a short period of time, and then take a break. How can you work toward a reading goal of forty-five minutes a day (experts practice for ninety minutes a day)? Remember that we read in this class for twenty minutes each day.

   Sample Goal: "I will read for thirty minutes at home each evening."

3. **Seek expert feedback.** This means that you have to have a great teacher or mentor or coach to help you. Think about the kinds of help you need to get better.

   Sample Goal: "I will ask my teacher to help me with a specific reading skill I wish to improve." (These are the skills we are practicing in the classroom— visualization, connection, question, monitor and repair, and analysis.)

4. **Take breaks to reflect on learning.** Relaxing after intense effort provides an opportunity to reflect, think about learning, and correct when necessary.

   Sample Goal: "I will write in my journal three days each week, reflecting on my reading enjoyment and what I am learning about improving my reading skill."

5. **Make mistakes, and then work to correct them.** Don't be afraid to make mistakes when you are practicing. The key is to learn from mistakes and not repeat them.

   Sample Goal: "If I choose a book that I do not enjoy reading, I will stop reading, return the book, and think about what I can do to choose a better one."

Sources: Schwarzt (2010) & Cobb (2010)

Figure 6.13 Quarter One Goal-Setting Sheet for Deliberate Practice

Set two goals that you will work on for this first quarter. Think about the goals that will best help you move forward toward reading excellence.

Goal One: _____

_____

_____

Specific Steps I Need to Take in Order to Accomplish Goal One:

_____

_____

_____

_____

_____

_____

_____

_____

Goal Two: _____

_____

_____

Specific Steps I Need to Take in Order to Accomplish Goal Two:

_____

_____

_____

_____

_____

_____

_____

_____

Authentic Audience Lesson Plan

Instructional Objectives for Students:

- Respond to thought-provoking prompts.

- Analyze other student responses.

- Write to a specific authentic audience including both a summary of other perspectives and their own evaluation of the issue.

- Develop critical-thinking skills.

- Strengthen their ability to write grammatically correct sentences.

Duration: Two to three sixty-minute class periods

Materials:

- Document camera or overhead projector with screen

- Computer connected to projector and Internet access

- Class sets of Figure 6.14, page 167, cut up for individual distribution

- Class set of Figure 6.15, page 168

- Student model letter Figure 6.16, page 169, perhaps as a class set

- TED Talk by Omar Ahmad from 2010 (www.ted.com/talks/omar_ahmad_political_change_with_pen_and_paper.html)

- For the optional extension activity, class set of Figure 6.17, page 170

Common Core English Language Arts Standards

Writing:

- Write arguments to support claim in an analysis of substantive topics or texts, using valid reasoning and relevant and sufficient evidence.

- Produce clear and coherent writing in which the development, organization, and style are appropriate to the task, purpose, and audience.

- Write routinely over extended time frames (time for research, reflection, and revision) and shorter time frames (a single sitting or a day or two) for a range of tasks, purposes, and audiences.

Procedure

First Day:

1. The teacher tells students that for the next few days, they will be investigating *advice* and *opinion* writing. After writing these words on the whiteboard, he or she asks students to think about what they mean and then to discuss the difference with partners. After students talk briefly, definitions and examples are shared with the class.

2. The teacher shows the class some funny teacher clips, like the ones at www.larryferlazzo.edublogs.org/2012/08/08/help-me-find-funny-clips-of-bad-teachers-like-this-one.

3. The teacher then tells students that they will be responding to a series of writing prompts where they will be sharing their opinions or advice on topics that directly apply to their daily classroom experiences in school. The teacher will need to place the prompts from Figure 6.14 on half sheets for distribution.

4. The teacher passes out the first prompt and displays it using the document camera. The teacher models what he or she would write and then asks students to write for three minutes.

5. As students are finishing, the teacher distributes the next prompt and collects the first Each set of finished prompts is put into a neat pile for later use. This continues until all prompts have been answered. The teacher can choose to reduce the number of prompts, if needed. We have found that with these prompts, the level of engagement is high and students are able to write to all ten.

Second Day:

1. The teacher reminds students of the writing they did the previous day and explains that they will now be reading one another's writing and will need to come up with a good summary of what the class thinks about one of the prompts presented. The teacher then passes out Figure 6.15 and discusses what students will be recording as they read through their classmates' ideas.

2. Teacher then numbers students one through ten, and students move to work with their groups (all the ones sit together, all the twos sit together, etc.) The teacher then passes out the sorted student responses (student responses to prompt one are given to the ones, student responses to prompt two are given to the twos, etc.)

3. Students are told to read each response and then pass their classmates' writing to their partner(s), taking notes of key ideas and/or quotes on their note-taking sheet. They need to read as many student responses as possible, so the teacher needs to circulate and ensure that students are reading and then passing.

4. After filling in key ideas from all the student responses, students need to come up with a summary statement for the overall class opinion on this issue. The teacher should give about ten minutes for the passing and recording and then give groups three to five minutes to develop summary statements. Groups then share their summaries aloud.

Third Day:

1. The teacher begins by telling students that today they will be writing letters to their teachers to inform and advise them on the issue they summarized in their small groups. Students could be given the options of writing a letter to one of their teachers; writing individual letters to all of their teachers; or writing one letter addressing a group of teachers. The key is for the audience to represent real people who will take the time to read the students' letters and maybe even respond to them.

2. The teacher then poses this question to the class: "If someone wanted to tell you to change, how should he or she present ideas so that you would listen and not get angry or offended?" The teacher makes a list of advice from students.

3. The teacher then writes these four words on the board (TAPS):

   o Topic

   o Audience

   o Purpose

   o Speaker

   Within the context of writing these letters to teachers, the teacher leads a group discussion on what these words mean.

   o For topic, each group will have a different topic, so the teacher will list off some examples like "what pushes my thinking is ..." or "I hate it when teachers ..."

   o For audience, the teacher will help steer conversation toward what students know of their teachers, thinking of ways to best get them to listen to their advice.

   o For purpose, the teachers asks: "What do you hope to achieve with this letter?"

   o For speaker, the teacher guides students to present themselves in a way that will make them look knowledgeable and serious about their issue. The teacher asks: "What kind of language should you use? How should you organize the piece? What kind of planning should you do first?"

4. The teacher reviews proper letter-writing format on the document camera, modeling the beginning of the letter, closure, etc., and then gives students about forty-five minutes to write. The teacher can also show the student model letter (Figure 6.16).

5. The teacher collects letters and distributes them to all teachers, or just to trusted colleagues instead. The teacher will need to use his/her judgment after reviewing the letters if all should be distributed or not. As an option, you can have teachers write back to students, responding to ideas, opinions, and advice presented.

6. Optional, if teacher would like to show video clip from TED series (Omar Ahmad: Political change with pen and paper, 2010, http://www.ted.com/talks/omar_ahmad_political_change_with_pen_and_paper.html), students can then discuss the value of letter writing and how this can benefit them both with the current assignment, and then later in life. Then ask students to add to the list previously created about how to pose advice for change so that someone will listen.

Assessment

- The letters should provide an easily assessable product.

- If desired, teachers could develop their own rubrics for use with this activity. See "The Best Rubric Sites (And A Beginning Discussion About Their Use)" (www.larryferlazzo.edublogs.org/2010/09/18/the-best-rubric-sites-and-a-beginning-discussion-about-their-use) for multiple free online tools for creating rubrics.

Extension Activity

- The teacher asks students to help him or her directly in this class by writing one more letter, this one addressed only to him or her. Acknowledging that they do so much reading and writing in this class, the teacher asks students to think about what motivates them to read and write. The teacher then distributes Figure 6.17 and reads through the example, asking students to highlight sections that they like or find interesting. The teacher then gives students thirty to forty minutes to compose a letter addressing these ideas.

- Throughout the remainder of the year, the teacher can make modifications to his or her teaching practice and credit specific students for those changes. This creates an open environment for students to feel respected as writers and academics.

Figure 6.14 Student Writing Prompts

1. Things that foster positive behavior are …

2. Teachers who keep us interested tend to …

3. Consequences that work are …

4. Homework that helps is …

5. Grading that works is …

6. I'll work harder if …

7. When I don't get it, _____ helps.

8. Ways to make difficult material easier to understand are …

9. What pushes my thinking is …

10. I hate it when teachers …

Figure 6.15 Note-Taking Sheet

Key Ideas and Quotes From Student Writing:	My Reaction and Opinion:

Summary Statement of Overall Class Opinion:

Figure 6.16   Student Model Letter A

Dear Construction and Design Teachers,

I appreciate all that you guys do for us students, but sometimes you guys can over do it. Most of the time teachers do great things for their students and some of the time they just annoy us to death.

The thing that teachers do that annoys students the most is when they invade our personal space. For example, when a student is writing or doing their work, sometimes teachers like to stand over them and stare at their work. It makes us feel very uncomfortable and awkward. Students also really hate it when teachers talk too much. For example, sometimes teachers tend to go on and on about something while students sit at their desks and day dream. I speak from experience.

Honestly, I think all students feel the same about teachers. We just want a teacher that will listen to us and help us achieve. We want nothing more, and nothing less. I believe that a good teacher takes their time to make sure everyone is on track. A good teacher encourages their students and trusts them. I hate it when teachers immediately assume that we are cheating just because we are talking or asking each other questions.

My advice to teachers is to simply give us more freedom and trust us a little more. At least let us pick our own seats. You guys get to control what we have to do, when we can go to the restroom, and how we do things. Most teachers would say, "Students can't control themselves," but that is not true. If only teachers can see through the eyes of a student they would understand.

Sincerely,

Gila Vang

Figure 6.17 Student Model Letter B

Dear Ms. Z,

What really motivates me to write is how it makes me feel after writing down what I feel. In middle school my teacher first got me to read a lot of books. She really got me into reading books. My favorite types of books are poetry, troubled teens, ex-gang member's life stories and people in prison. I don't know what I like about these kinds of books. All I can say is that I really like reading stuff that starts out with violence and a strong meaning behind it. Poetry books are really great, too. I really enjoy getting ideas and things from them. They're a big part of my life, but I have to say that my poetry is the most valuable to me because I can express myself more openly.

    I really thank my 8th grade teacher a lot because she was the person who really got me started on poetry. One day we were just writing whatever we felt and she told me to write whatever was on my mind so I did. After she read what I wrote she asked if we can some way make it into a poem so I did. I wrote my first poem that very day called "My Pain." I really didn't care for it much at first but then I realized how relieved I felt after reading it our loud. It showed me that whatever problems you're having or situations that are going on, you can't really talk to anybody. Just write them down because it's better to let them out on paper instead of keeping them in your head. Just let your mind explore into places that you never thought you can go and eventually you'll create a masterpiece.

                       Sincerely,

                       Santiago Marin

Chapter 7

How Can You Best

Prepare Students for Standardized Tests While Doing No Harm to Them?

So much rides on the results of standardized tests these days. They're even talking about making student scores worth 50 percent of my own evaluation and using them to determine my pay! I don't want to spend weeks "drilling and killing" my students with test-prep work sheets. What am I supposed to do?

Much has been written about the many problems with high-stakes standardized tests (Darling-Hammond, 2007; Popham, n.d.; Ravitch, 2010). A paper coauthored by Netta Weinstein and Richard Ryan (2010), one of world's premier researchers on motivation, has listed a few of the problems resulting from high-stakes testing, including "teaching to the test, narrowing of curricula, [and] crowding out of enriching student activities" (p. 230). A 2011 report from the National Academy of Sciences also criticized the negative impact high-stakes testing has had on student learning (Sparks, 2011a).

Ted Appel, principal at Luther Burbank High School in Sacramento, California, has characterized test results as being useful for being "data-informed," but cautions against using them to be "data-driven" (Ferlazzo, 2009, August 26). If schools are data-driven, they might make decisions like keeping students who are almost ready to take a higher level of math in algebra so that the school does well on the algebra state test. Or, in English, teachers might focus a lot of energy on teaching a strand that is heavily emphasized on the tests—even though it might not help students become lifelong readers. In other words, schools can tend to focus on their institutional self-interest instead of what's best for the students. In schools that are data-informed, test results are just one more piece of information that can be helpful in determining future directions.

The theme of this book is helping students develop intrinsic motivation and life skills that will help them become better learners and more equipped to deal with challenges in and outside of school, now and in the future. Becoming better at taking standardized tests is nowhere near as important as developing greater self-control, a stronger ability to cope with stress, and a willingness to look at problems and mistakes as opportunities to learn. (Fortunately, at least some of the strategies discussed in this chapter can be applied by students in venues apart from taking standardized tests.) Nevertheless, we live, as community organizers say, in the world as it is, not in the world as we would like it to be, and high-stakes standardized tests are a reality. Given this fact, besides being the best teachers we can be during the year (as well as being advocates of reducing or eliminating standardized test use and replacing it with more effective evaluation tools, such as teacher-developed assessments and student portfolios), what are the most effective and ethical ways we can help prepare our students to do their best on these tests?

This chapter offers strategies, research, and suggestions to teachers on how they can provide test prep. It shares research-based evidence that teachers can use to oppose more common disruptive and time-intensive test prep activities that are prevalent in many schools today. The hope behind this chapter is that we teachers will do no harm to our students, while at the same time assisting them to bring their best efforts to the task—and, perhaps, learn a few strategies that might help them successfully prepare for other challenging situations in their lives. The ideas here are designed to make test prep and taking tests less demeaning, distressing, and depressing exercises—to teachers and to students—than they are so often today.

This chapter, as most others in this book, is divided into two parts—immediate responses for the day of a test and setting-the-stage ideas for the time leading up to the test, along with a lesson plan. Though some of the details in this chapter specifically relate to tests in the English language arts, most of the suggestions can be applied or modified in other subject areas.

Research shows that at least 15 percent, and possibly as much as 30 percent, of a test taker's success could depend on his or her motivation and other ambiguous factors (Guthrie, 2002, p. 374). Both sections in this chapter provide ideas on how teachers can ethically help increase the odds that students maximize their potential in these "factors."

Immediate Responses

Writing About a Successful Personal Experience, a Successful Person, or Looking at His or Her Image

Asking students to take a minute or two prior to the test to write about a successful personal experience (Nelson & Knight, 2010), or to write about another successful person like a professor (Gladwell, 2005, p. 56) has resulted in higher test scores.

My personal favorite activity in this category is to give students five minutes to respond to this prompt: *Think about one of your ancestors, and write about one or more successes he or she had in life. Write a few sentences about the person, and draw a picture that represents him or her, and/or his or her success.*

Then, after a few minutes, I have them share with a partner, which incorporates the next activity described in this chapter—having a conversation.

This ancestor exercise builds on research that found having students spend a few minutes just thinking about ancestors—deceased or alive—or writing about them prior to taking a standardized test will result in greater effort and better results. The researchers concluded that thinking about the success of those with whom we are genetically connected, and the problems that they have overcome, makes us believe that we have similar qualities (Fischer, Sauer, Vogrincic, & Weisweiler, 2010).

An additional benefit of this ancestor exercise is teachers can learn some amazing things about students and their families. Here are a few condensed examples of what students have written:

♦ *My auntie finally finished her college years.*

♦ *My mom's grandmother's mom was a slave and was alive when slavery ended. She got to celebrate, and even if she hadn't anywhere to go it was a special moment for her.*

♦ *My dad got to America. He got papers.*

♦ *My grandpa was born in Mexico and grew up there. Growing up he messed around with ropes because he loved the style, so he got really good and great with horses. He never lost a match. It's about how many you catch and you have is a horse and a rope.*

♦ *One good, successful person that I know is my dad. I think that he is a successful person because when something bad happens in our family he always knows what to do.*

♦ *My grandfather was a CIA soldier. That was one of his success because he helped Americans during the Vietnam War.*

Lastly, girls just seeing images of famous women scientists on the walls has resulted in higher science scores (Berreby, 2010). Though research has not yet been undertaken to explore the additional implications of these study results, it certainly couldn't hurt to place images of successful scientists and professionals representing different ethnic groups and genders around the classroom.

The research behind these strategies can be explained to students so they can use it to prepare for future high-stakes activities.

Having Students Talk With One Another for a Few Minutes

Dividing the class into pairs and having them talk about a social issue for ten minutes prior to a test has been found to result in higher scores. This kind of social interaction and building of "social capital" increased mental processing speed and working memory, according to researchers ("Ten Minutes of Talking," 2007). It appears to warm up the brain, especially areas like working memory and concentration, which are used in both social engagement and taking a test.

Students could possibly determine their own topics and partners prior to testing day to facilitate the process. Though the social issue discussed in the experiment was a current event, it appears that researchers believe that any topic of mutual interest and that can be sustained for ten minutes would achieve the same effect as long as it took place between friends (Ybarra et al., 2008).

Another study found that just asking participants to spend eight minutes getting to know another person produced similar results (Shea, 2010).

Again, teachers can explain the research behind this activity and discuss it as a tool that students could use in preparing for future challenging situations.

Providing Snacks and Water to Students

Researchers have found that providing students with peppermints on test days has resulted in higher scores. It is thought that they both provide glucose for the brain (Jensen, 2010) and that their odor somehow increases student attention (Aratani, 2007).

Glucose, in reasonable amounts, can enhance memory (Jensen, 2012). Other studies have reported similar results when students chewed gum during tests (Whitson, n.d.). Those studies, however, were financed by the Wrigley Gum company, which might raise suspicion. More recent research indicates that if chewing gum does indeed provide a cognitive boost, it is probably very short-lived (Willingham, 2012).

Drinking a cup of water twenty minutes prior to taking a test has also had positive results. Researchers are not exactly sure why test results improved, but others suggest that students being better hydrated is an important reason for the improvement (Black, 2009).

Once again, in addition to potentially providing food and/or water to students on test day, teachers can explain their effect on performance and students can consider getting them on their own in the future—prior to tests and other times when they want to be as focused as possible.

Test-Taking Stress

Some of us, including students, just don't do well in high-pressure situations like taking tests. Researchers have found that having students write about their test-taking thoughts and worries for ten minutes prior to the start of the exam "canceled out the negative effects of test anxiety" ("Writing About Exam," n.d.). The researchers believe that putting the worries on paper helped clear the working memory of clutter that would disrupt cognitive functions.

Telling students about this activity and the research behind it could also provide them with a tool they could use prior to any potentially high-stress activity that would require a large amount of intellectual energy—a job interview, an oral presentation, etc.

Posting the Letter A on Classroom Walls

A study has found that just placing the letter A or A+ and other positive signs on classroom walls increases student achievement on standardized tests. The researchers wrote:

> Adorning classrooms with symbols of achievement, such as A+ and other success-oriented words and phrases may activate effort, pride, and the intention to perform well in a standardized testing situation. ("Exposure to Letters," 2010)

According to the researchers, the signs primed students' subconscious to succeed. (Before using these signs, teachers should check the rules in their state regarding what is acceptable to post on classroom walls.) This kind of priming is also the reasoning behind the next suggestion (sentence scrambles) in this section ("Priming the Customer," 2006). Priming is not thought to increase intelligence. Instead, it appears to possibly enhance the ability of people to focus their abilities more effectively over a short period of time.

Many researchers believe that priming does not work if you know that it is occurring (Carey, 2007). However, recent studies have found that telling ill people they are receiving placebos (fake medication) still results in health improvement for many (Hamzelou, 2010). This finding provides some evidence for the belief that telling people about priming may not result in eliminating its effect. There are ethical issues in using priming on students without telling them (though, perhaps, not as many as there are in spending countless hours in test preparation). Given that concern, I have chosen to tell students in advance about the research behind any brain-priming activity. The two mentioned in this chapter—the success signs discussed previously and the sentence scrambles in the next section—take so little time and energy that even if they don't help, they certainly can't hurt.

And, assuming there are no state prohibitions on it, students can also create their own success-oriented signs that are particularly meaningful to them. Even if there are state restrictions against them during tests, there is no reason that these can't be posted during the rest of the year!

Ed Tech
Making Inspirational Posters

Students could make inspirational posters for placement around the classroom on test day—if allowed by state testing regulations. They can include the grade A as mentioned earlier in this chapter, or anything else they feel would be helpful. Motivator (www.bighugelabs.com/motivator.php) is an easy site to use for creating posters.

Completing Sentence Scrambles

Sentence scrambles are groups of words in a sentence placed in the incorrect order, which students have to write in the correct order. Malcolm Gladwell (2005) has cited experiments using sentence scrambles to prime the brain to perform certain behaviors (though not specifically for test taking) (p. 52).

The studies could be applied to tests, however. Students could be given several sentence scrambles related to success ("I will do well on the test" or "I will work hard on the test and be successful") to use in a short game prior to test taking.

Setting the Stage

Taking the Test in the Same Place Students Have Learned

This idea is obviously one for the test day itself, but it is in this section because of the prior logistical work involved in making it happen. Studies have shown that student stress is increased if the test is taken in a new environment, but lessened if taken in the location where the learning took place. The same studies suggest that even if that is not possible, just taking students to the test location for a test review a few days earlier can help mitigate the increased levels of stress (Jensen, 2010).

Administrators at Luther Burbank High School in Sacramento, California, manage the herculean task of rearranging class schedules for six days and organizing test booklets so that all students take every test with their subject teacher, in the classroom where they've been studying that subject every day, with their usual classmates. In other words, students will take the English test in their regular English class (which has been expanded to three hours for that day).

How Much Time Should You Spend on Test Preparation, and What Should You do?

"Test-wiseness"—familiarity with the format of the test and test-taking strategies—has been found to comprise between 10 percent and 25 percent of the difference between student test scores (again, these results are for English language arts tests, but there is no reason to think other subject areas would be substantially different). As mentioned earlier, motivation was between 15 percent and 30 percent. By far, however, the largest factors were content knowledge and reading strategies—in other words, the daily curriculum that is ordinarily taught in the classroom (Guthrie, 2002, p. 374).

Preparation in test-taking skills has been found in the vast majority of research to result in higher test scores. An older study cited by some pre-packaged test preparation programs ("Research-Based Test Preparation," n.d.) recommends as many as twenty to thirty hours of preparation in test-wiseness (Berliner & Casanova, 1993). However more recent studies, in the words of researcher John T. Guthrie (2002), recommend that this kind of test prep "should be a few days, but never weeks or months. It will be counterproductive if this time allocation is excessive" (p. 387). Guthrie recommends allocating test-preparation time proportionally to represent the factors that affect test results—a smaller proportion in enhancing motivation and test-wiseness, and the vast majority in what could be considered the regular curriculum.

> Test prep "should be a few days, but never weeks or months."
>
> —John T. Guthrie

The "Test-Wiseness Lesson Plan" that follows reflects that perspective with a four- or five-day unit spread over the three weeks prior to a standardized test. More than that amount can result in students feeling overwhelmed and focusing on remembering too many test-taking techniques rather than reading strategies and content knowledge.

Could spending much more time on intensive and direct test preparation in certain circumstances conceivably result in higher test scores for some students? Of course that's a possibility. Teachers and administrators, however, would need to consider if doing so is in the long-term best interest of all their students.

A study released in 2012 that received a great deal of public attention found that though many kinds of usual tasks used for intensive "test prep," such as extrinsic motivation and memorization, might result in short-term assessment gains, it was an emphasis on the development of intrinsic motivation and deeper learning strategies (summarizing, explaining, making connections, etc.) that led to *long-term* academic growth. In fact, the study found that the usual "test" prep techniques actually hurt long-term achievement (Murayama & Pekrun, 2012, p. 11).

Test-Wiseness Lesson Plan

Instructional Objectives for Students:

- Identify goals for upcoming standardized tests.

- Learn test-taking strategies.

- Learn academic vocabulary and practice test questions related to ongoing class curriculum.

Duration: Five 55-minute class periods over a three-week period

Materials:

- Student copies of Figure 7.1, page 186. Note that the figure is a sample using California state test figures, and that teachers should use the data relevant to their state.

- Student copies of Figure 7.2, page 187. Note that the figure is a sample, and that teachers should review the officially released practice versions from their state and develop a more relevant list.

- Student copies of a teacher-developed mini-test using questions in all the test formats, and using curriculum that has been taught in the class during the previous few months

- Printouts showing state test scores from at least two previous years for each student

- Overhead projector, document camera, or whiteboard

- Materials needed for curriculum-related activity students will work on independently during the two or so days of individual conversations—for example, a video or poster activity

- Seven or eight small whiteboards, markers, and erasers. One hundred sheets of 8½" x 11" paper and seven markers would work as a substitute.

- Small poster paper and colored markers or pencils

- One copy of Figure 7.3, page 187

Common Core English Language Arts Standards

Reading: Determine central ideas or themes of a text and analyze their development; summarize the key supporting details and ideas.

Speaking and Listening:

- Prepare for and participate effectively in a range of conversations and collaborations with diverse partners, building on others' ideas and expressing their own clearly and persuasively.

- Adapt speech to a variety of contexts and communicative tasks, demonstrating command of formal English when indicated or appropriate.

Language:

- Demonstrate command of the conventions of standard English grammar and usage when writing or speaking.

- Demonstrate command of the conventions of standard English capitalization, punctuation, and spelling when writing.

Procedure

First and Second Days:

(three weeks prior to the test; as much as two 50-minute class periods, but probably less)

1. Teacher announces that state tests will take place three weeks from now. He or she writes on the board:

    Do you think it's important to try your best on your test? If so, why? If not, why not?

    The teacher asks students to take out a piece of paper and write an answer to the question. After a few minutes, students divide into pairs and share their answers with a partner. Afterward, the teacher calls on a few students to share what they wrote (after having circulated in the room during the sharing and having identified students to call upon).

2. The teacher announces that while students are working on an independent activity—reading silently, watching a video, working on a cooperative learning project, etc.—he or she will call students over to his or her desk individually to talk about the upcoming state tests. (These five-minute individual conversations can also happen over a period of a few days.) The teacher explains that since the class uses goals a lot (see Chapter 1), they will also be making goals for these tests, and he or she will show them their scores from last year.

3. The teacher calls up each student and tells the student his or her scores from the previous two years to help students set realistic goals for this year.

The teacher could begin a conversation this way:

> "Students made a lot of good points when they just shared why it's important to do your best on the tests. Also, the test results, along with grades, are going to be the first impressions your teachers next year are going to have of you—before they actually meet you face-to-face. And first impressions can last awhile. I question whether these tests are an accurate measure of someone's ability, but even I find myself prejudging students before I meet them based on their grades and test scores. And the same holds true if you move and switch schools. I don't believe that test scores are accurate assessments of your intelligence, but I do think that they can sometimes indicate how well someone can concentrate—his or her self-discipline. It's difficult sitting down for an hour and a half taking one of these tests; you might start to run out of time with twenty more questions left to answer and be very tempted to not spend much time on those remaining, or even just bubble them all in quickly. I certainly did that when I was in school."

The teacher can then ask students their ideas on how they could get into the mind-set of approaching the last twenty questions with the same energy level as the first twenty—going to the bathroom, getting a drink of water, stretching, visualizing, etc.

Research has found that grit (in other words, perseverance) is the most accurate indicator of success in life. Princeton neuroscientist Sam Wang has described taking standardized tests as an opportunity for students to build up and demonstrate their perseverance (Gots, 2011). During the one-on-one conversations with students, the teacher can make the connection between grit and taking the test. It might be one of the few positive learning opportunities provided by these high-stakes standardized assessments.

4. The teacher then tells the student their scores from the previous two years (It might not be a good idea to show students the official printouts because they often also show the label the scores give—such as far below basic, below basic, etc. That is the reason the sample goal sheet includes the numbers in each level, but not the names.)

5. The teacher then gives the student Figure 7.1. He or she asks the student to write down his or her score from last year in the appropriate space. The teacher points out the different levels, how far that particular student is from moving up to the next level, and how much each question is worth. The teacher asks the student what he or she thinks would be a reasonable goal for this year, and how many additional questions he or she would need to

answer correctly. (Oftentimes, it is a matter of answering just one or two more questions correctly.) The teacher then explains to the student that the class will do some test-preparation activities over the next few weeks that will help him or her answer the other questions on the form, and during that time students will need to complete this form and have it signed by their parents. The form will be due in two weeks, but can be turned in sooner. The teacher asks the student for ideas on how to meet his or her goal (the student should be able to remember some of the ideas the class just discussed—taking a break, etc., as well as trying to be focused in class between now and then) and why he or she wants to meet the goal (again, the student should be able to list some ideas from the discussion), and suggests the student write those ideas on Figure 7.1.

6. The teacher continues the same process with each student.

Third Day:
(two weeks prior to the test; one 50-minute class period)

1. The teacher reminds students that their goal sheets (Figure 7.1) will be due in one week.

2. The teacher explains that students will review important test words using a game. He or she places a list of words that were determined important based on previously released test versions (similar to the one in Figure 7.2) and says each word.

3. He or she explains that students will get into groups of four or five students each. When the game begins, students will organize their groups in a circle. Each person in the group will be given a dictionary, and the group will have 10 minutes to write a definition for each word that is understandable—sometimes that might mean just copying down the definition in the dictionary, and sometimes they might have to put it in their own words. Everyone in the group will have to have written down the definitions for all the words, and the teacher will collect them at the end of class. If desired, after a few minutes, the teacher can extend the time to 15 minutes.

4. Next, the teacher collects all the dictionaries and distributes one small whiteboard, marker, and eraser (or 15 blank sheets of paper and a marker) to each group. He or she will either call out a word or say a definition, and each group will have 30 seconds to write down the answer on the whiteboard or sheet. Once the groups have written down their answers, they should leave them facedown until the teacher tells people to raise them. Each group will get one point for a correct answer.

5. The teacher continues the game until all words are reviewed, though it would be good to repeat words by asking their definition and vice versa.

Groups can bet as many of their point as they want for the final question, which should be related to the test but not vocabulary. It might be something like: "How many points is each question worth on the test?" or "Name two reasons why it is important to do well on the test."

6. The teacher gives the winning group some sort of simple reward or prize and collects the word definitions.

Fourth Day:

(one week prior to the state test; one-50 minute class period)

1. The teacher collects the signed and completed goal sheets

2. The teacher explains that he or she would like to review some test-taking tips. He or she asks students to take a minute to think about what tricks or strategies have helped them succeed in previous state tests, and to write them down. Then, the teacher asks students to share with a partner. Next, using a document camera or easel paper, he or she asks students to share some of their ideas and writes them down.

3. If any of the tips listed in Figure 7.3 are not shared by students, the teacher should add them. Do not give students copies of Figure 7.3, however; it is better for them to come up with most of the tips on their own. The teacher can elaborate on some, especially "Eliminate wrong answers and make your best guess." The teacher can give an example using this question: "How old am I?" He or she can list "10" as one answer and "100" as another, and then the other two choices can be the accurate age and one that is ten years younger or older. The teacher can lead students through a process of elimination that increases the odds of their choosing the correct answer even if they are not sure. To lightheartedly support this strategy, he or she might want to quote Arthur Conan Doyle (2012), who said: "How often have I said to you that when you have eliminated the impossible, whatever remains … must be the truth" (p. 54).

4. The teacher asks students to copy down the list of strategies. While they are doing so, he or she can distribute a few sample teacher-created questions using the test format that cover topics studied recently in the curriculum. He or she asks students to answer the questions.

5. After fifteen or twenty minutes, the teacher asks students to share their answers with a partner, as well as if they used any of the test-taking tips to arrive at them.

6. The teacher then leads a short class discussion about the sample test, and asks students to turn in their list of test-taking tips and their sample tests.

Fifth Day:

(two days prior to the test)

1. The teacher returns student goal sheets, test-taking tips, vocabulary sheets, and sample tests.

2. The teacher explains that each student should choose three vocabulary words and one test-taking tip. Each student will make a small poster on an 8½" x 11" sheet for each one they choose. Students should write the word or tip on the top, and then illustrate it. The teacher should show a model. Students will be given 30 minutes to make the simple posters.

3. After thirty minutes, desks will be put into two rows facing each other. Students will have one minute each to show their posters to the student facing them until the teacher says "Next!" and one side moves down a seat. The class uses this "speed-dating" process for 15 minutes.

4. In the remaining class minutes, the teacher explains that he or she wants each student to staple all their test-prep materials into a packet with a cover sheet they can label "Test-Prep" and decorate if they want. The teacher should write on the whiteboard the order which the packet should be in—cover sheet, goal sheet, vocabulary, test-prep tips, sample test, and posters. The teacher collects all the packets at the end of the class period. If students want to take the packets home to redo any parts of them, they can for return on the following day.

Sixth Day:

(one day prior to the test; one 50-minute class period)

1. The teacher explains that students are going to play a game similar to the one they did the previous week. This time, however, they will not have anything to look at where they can find the answers. They will have five (or ten) minutes to study their test-tip packets after the teacher returns them. They can study them individually or with partners. At the end of that time, the teacher will collect the packets, and students will divide into groups of four or five students each to play the game.

2. At the end of five or ten minutes, the teacher collects the student packets. Students then divide into groups, and the game proceeds as it did in the third day.

3. The teacher returns test-tip packets to students and tells them he or she will collect them on the day of the test.

Assessment

The teacher can create a detailed rubric for the student test-tip packet that is appropriate for the classroom situation. See "The Best Rubric Sites (And A Beginning Discussion About Their Use)" (www.larryferlazzo.edublogs.org/2010/09/18/the-best-rubric-sites-and-a-beginning-discussion-about-their-use) for multiple free online tools for creating rubrics.

Ed Tech
Online Test Practice

There are numerous free online practice sites for state assessments. Teachers might want to bring their students to the computer lab for a day of practice. You can find a list of sites at "A Beginning 'The Best ...' List Of Free & Decent Online Practice Sites For State Tests—Help Me Add More!" (www.larryferlazzo.edublogs.org/2010/08/02/a-beginning-the-best-list-of-free-decent-online-practice-sites-for-state-tests-help-me-add-more/). Even though you might not find one there for your state, others might still be similar.

Figure 7.1 State Test Goal Sheet

Name _____

Class _____

| English | 150–262 | 263–299 | 300–349 | 350–400 | 401–600 |

Each question is worth approximately 5–8 points.

- My score last year in English was _____.
- My goal in English this year is _____.
- In order to achieve that goal I have to answer _____ more questions correctly.
- I will do this by (list ideas of what you can do between now and the test, and what you can do during the test itself):

   1. _____

     _____

   2. _____

     _____

   3. _____

     _____

   4. _____

     _____

- I want to achieve this goal because:

   5. _____

     _____

   6. _____

     _____

   7. _____

     _____

   8. _____

     _____

_____   _____
Student Signature   Parent Signature

Figure 7.2 Important Test Words and Terms

narrator	tone	primary
figurative language	compare	personification
except	contrast	traditional
consistent	negative	tradition
denotation	tendency	excerpt
connotation	recurring	rhetorical
similar	influenced	logically
theme	assumes	
author's purpose	persuasive	

Figure 7.3 Tips for Being "Test Wise"

- Read each question carefully and more than once.
- Read the questions before you read any other part of the prompt.
- Underline important words in the text as you read.
- Answer easy questions first.
- Skip the hard questions and come back to them later (put a mark in your test booklet next to the ones you skip).
- Eliminate wrong answers and make your best guess.
- If you want to change an answer, be sure to erase the first one completely.
- Make sure you are bubbling in the answer on the correct number.
- It's okay to take a few thirty-second breaks during the test if you get tired. Just shutting your eyes and taking a few deep breaths can help keep you alert.

Sources: Millman & Pauk (1969), Amer (2007), & STAR/CST tips and scoring chart (n.d.)

You may have heard this tip before, which isn't on the list: "Trust yourself; your first guess is usually the best." Here's why that recommendation isn't a good one:

> Even though first answers are often correct, you shouldn't be afraid to change your original answer if, upon reflection, it seems wrong to you. Dozens of studies over the past 70 years have found that students who change dubious answers usually improve their test scores. For example, a May, 2005, study of 1,561 introductory psychology midterm exams found that when students changed their answers, they went from wrong to right 51% of the time, right to wrong 25% of the time, and wrong to a different wrong answer 23% of the time. (Plous, 2013)

Afterword

The challenges listed in this book, and the ideas that are offered as ways to respond, are obviously just a drop in the bucket of the many issues that classroom teachers and their students face every day.

If you have other challenges that you and your colleagues are confronting, share them at www.larryferlazzo.edublogs.org/contact-me. And if you have ideas on how to effectively respond to common classroom problems, please consider sharing them there as well.

References

10 psychological effects of nonsexual touch. (n.d.). *Psyblog*. Retrieved from http://www.spring.org.uk/2011/04/10-psychological-effects-of-nonsexual-touch.php?utm_source=feedburner&utm_medium=feed&utm_campaign=Feed%3A+PsychologyBlog+%28PsyBlog%29

A picture is worth a thousand thoughts: Inquiry with Bloom's taxonomy. (n.d.). Retrieved from http://www.learnnc.org/lp/media/articles/bloom0405-3/bloompix.html

Ahmad, Omar. (2010, February). Omar Ahmad: Political change with pen and paper. *TED*. Retrieved from http://www.ted.com/talks/omar_ahmad_political_change_with_pen_and_paper.html

Akil, B., II. (2009, November 9). How the Navy Seals increased passing rates. *Psychology Today*. Retrieved from http://www.psychologytoday.com/blog/communication-central/200911/how-the-navy-seals-increased-passing-rates

Aldous, R. (2007). *The lion and the unicorn*. New York, NY: W. W. Norton.

Alfieri, L., Brooks, P. J., Aldrich, N. J., & Tenenbaum, H. R. (2011). Does discovery-based instruction enhance learning? *Journal of Educational Psychology, 103*(1), 1–18. Retrieved from http://psycnet.apa.org/index.cfm?fa=buy.optionToBuy&id=2010-23599-001

Amabile, T., & Kramer, S. (2011). *The progress principle: Using small wins to ignite joy, engagement, and creativity at work*. Boston, MA: Harvard Business Review Press.

Amer, A. A. (2007). EFL/ESL test-wiseness and test-taking strategies. (ERIC Document Reproduction No. ED497399). Retrieved from http://www.eric.ed.gov/PDFS/ED497399.pdf

American Academy of Child and Adolescent Psychiatry. (2005, May). Helping teenagers with stress. Retrieved from http://www.aacap.org/cs/root/facts_for_families/helping_teenagers_with_stress

American Psychological Association. (2011, April 26). Power and choice are interchangeable: It's all about controlling your life. *ScienceDaily*. Retrieved from http://www.sciencedaily.com/releases/2011/04/110426111419.htm

Anderson, A. (2012, February 22). Guest post – Look at the camera and say "think." [Web log post] Retrieved from http://www.freetech4teachers.com/2012/02/guest-post-look-at-camera-and-say-think.html?utm_source=feedburner

&utm_medium=feed&utm_campaign=Feed%3A+freetech4teachers%2Fc
GEY+%28Free+Technology+for+Teachers%29&utm_content=Google+Reader

Aratani, L. (2007, March 20). The power of peppermint is put to the test. *The Washington Post*. Retrieved from http://www.washingtonpost.com/wpdyn/content/article/2007/03/19/AR2007031901624.html

Ariely, D. (2012, May 26). Why we lie. *The Wall Street Journal*. Retrieved from http://online.wsj.com/article/SB10001424052702304840904577422090013997320.html?mod=WSJ_hpp_MIDDLENexttoWhatsNewsTop

Armstrong, D. (2009). The power of apology: How saying sorry can leave both patients and nurses feeling better. *Nursing Times*, 105(44), 16–19.

Askell-Williams, H., Lawson, M. J., & Skrzypiec, G. (2012). Scaffolding cognitive and metacognitive strategy instruction in regular class lessons. *Instructional Science*, 40(2), 413–443. doi: 10.1007/s11251-011-9182-5. Retrieved from http://www.springerlink.com/content/p068qm6808q5g075/

Ayres, I. (2011, January 21). The economics of tiger parenting. *Freakonomics*. Retrieved from http://www.freakonomics.com/2011/01/21/the-economics-of-tiger-parenting/?scp=5&sq=%2522motivation%2522&st=cse

Bailey, P. (2012, February 27). Metacognition – I know (or don't know) that I know. *BrainFacts.org*. Retrieved from http://www.brainfacts.org/sensing-thinking-behaving/awareness-and-attention/articles/2012/metacognition/

Barker, E. (2010, May 26). Does doodling make you smarter? *Barking up the wrong tree*. Retrieved from http://www.bakadesuyo.com/does-doodling-make-you-smarter?utm_source=feedburner&utm_medium=feed&utm_campaign=Feed:+bakadesuyo+(Barking+up+the+wrong+tree

Barker, E. (2011, November 12). Which is more persuasive: Scaring someone or encouraging them? *Barking up the wrong tree*. Retrieved from http://www.bakadesuyo.com/which-is-more-persuasive-scaring-someone-or-e?utm_source=feedburner&utm_medium=feed&utm_campaign=Feed%3A+bakadesuyo+%28Barking+up+the+wrong+tree%29&utm_content=Google+Reader

Beck, M. (2010, November 23). Thank you. No, thank you. *The Wall Street Journal*. Retrieved from http://online.wsj.com/article/SB10001424052748704244390457563054148629005s2.html?mod=WSJ_LifeStyle_LeadStoryNA#

Begley, S., & Chatzky, J. (2011, October 30). The new science behind your spending addiction. *The Daily Beast*. Retrieved from http://www.thedailybeast.com/newsweek/2011/10/30/the-new-science-behind-your-spending-addiction.html

The Benjamin Franklin effect. (2011, October 5). *You are not so smart: A celebration of self delusion*. Retrieved from http://youarenotsosmart.com/2011/10/05/the-benjamin-franklin-effect

Berliner, D. C., & Casanova, U. (1993). *Putting research to work in your school*. New York, NY: Scholastic Leadership Policy Research.

Berreby, D. (2010, May 26). To improve girls' science scores, show them women scientists. *Big Think*. Retrieved from http://bigthink.com/ideas/20260

Berten, H. (2008). *Peer influences on risk behavior: A network study of social influence on adolescents in Flemish secondary schools*. Paper presented at the Annual Meeting of the American Sociological Society, Boston, MA. Retrieved from http://www.allacademic.com/meta/p_mla_apa_research_citation/2/3/9/7/8/p239786_index.html

Best uses of independent reading time. (2011, July). *Best Practices Weekly*. Retrieved from http://bestpracticesweekly.com/wp-content/uploads/2011/07/Best-uses-of-independent-reading-time-Article.pdf

Black, R. (2009, March 12). Drinking water linked to higher test scores for kids: Study. *NYDailyNews.com*. Retrieved from http://www.nydailynews.com/life-style/health/drinking-water-linked-higher-test-scores-kids-study-article-1.371530

Blue, L. (2010, August 23). Could hand-washing boost your workplace productivity? *Time Healthland*. Retrieved from http://healthland.time.com/2010/08/23/can-hand-washing-boost-workplace-productivit/?utm_source=feedburner&utm_medium=email&utm_campaign=Feed:+timeblogs/wellness+(TIME:+Wellness)

Bluestein, J. (n.d.). *Alternatives to advice-giving: Ask, don't tell*. Retrieved from http://www.janebluestein.com/handouts/questions.html

Brief diversions vastly improve focus, researchers find. (2011, February 8). *Science Daily*. Retrieved from http://www.sciencedaily.com/releases/2011/02/110208131529.htm

British Columbia Teacher Librarians' Association. (2009, April). *Book levelling and school library collections*. Retrieved from http://bctf.ca/bctla/pub/documents/BookLevellingandSchoolLibraryCollections.pdf

Brody, J. E. (2012, May 21). A richer life by seeing the glass half full. *The New York Times*. Retrieved from http://well.blogs.nytimes.com/2012/05/21/a-richer-life-by-seeing-the-glass-half-full/

Bronson, P. (2007, February 11). How not to talk to your kids: The inverse power of praise. *New York Magazine*. Retrieved from http://nymag.com/news/features/27840/

Bronson, P. (2009, October 7). Motivation and flow: The teenager edition. *The Daily Beast*. Retrieved from http://www.thedailybeast.com/newsweek/blogs/nurture-shock/2009/10/07/motivation-and-flow-the-teenager-edition.html

Brooks, D. (2010, August 23). A case of mental courage. *The New York Times*. Retrieved from http://www.nytimes.com/2010/08/24/opinion/24brooks.html?_r=1&hp

Calkins, L., Ehrenworth, M., & Lehman, C. (2012). *Pathways to the Common Core: Accelerating achievement*. Portsmouth, NH: Heinemann.

Cardellichio, T., & Field, W. (1997). Seven strategies that encourage neural branching. *Educational Leadership*, 54(6), 33–36. Retrieved from http://www.ascd.org/publications/educational-leadership/mar97/vol54/num06/Seven-Strategies-That-Encourage-Neural-Branching.aspx

Carey, B. (2007, July 31). Who's minding the mind? *The New York Times*. Retrieved from http://www.nytimes.com/2007/07/31/health/psychology/31subl.html?_r=1&pagewanted=all

Carey, B. (2010, February 22). Evidence that little touches do mean so much. *The New York Times*. Retrieved from http://www.nytimes.com/2010/02/23/health/23mind.html?_r=2&em

Charan, R. (2012, June 21). The discipline of listening. *Harvard Business Review.* Retrieved from http://blogs.hbr.org/cs/2012/06/the_discipline_of_listen ing.html

Cobb, J. (2010, April). How do you get to Carnegie Hall? 8 keys to deliberative practice. *Mission to Learn.* Retrieved from http://www.missiontolearn. com/2010/04/deliberate-practice

Collective punishment. (n.d.). *Wikipedia.* Retrieved from http://en.wikipedia.org/ wiki/Collective_punishment

Csikszentmihalyi, M. (2004). Mihaly Csikszentmihalyi: Flow, the secret to happiness. *TED.* Retrieved from http://www.ted.com/talks/mihaly_csiksz entmihalyi_on_flow.html

Cuban, L. (2011, June 16). Jazz, basketball, and teacher decision-making. *Larry Cuban on school reform and classroom practice.* Retrieved from http://larrycuban. wordpress.com/2011/06/16/jazz-basketball-and-teacher-decision-making/

Dalai, R. S., & Bonaccio, S. (2010). What types of advice to decision-makers prefer? *Organizational Behavior and Human Decision Processes, 112*(1), 11–23. Retrieved from http://www.sciencedirect.com/science/article/pii/S0749597809001083

Darling-Hammond, L. (2007, October 14). High-quality standards, a curriculum based on critical thinking can enlighten our students. *SFGate.* Retrieved from http://www.sfgate.com/cgi-bin/article.cgi?f=/c/a/2007/10/14/MN9G SOEUC.DTL&hw=linda+hammond+darling&sn=001&sc=1000

De Posada, J. (2009, May). Joachim de Posada: Don't eat the marshmallow! *TED.* Retrieved from http://www.ted.com/talks/joachim_de_posada_says_don_t_ eat_the_marshmallow_yet.html

DiSalvo, D. (2010, January 10). Does making a public commitment really help people lose weight? *Neuronarrative.* Retrieved from http://neuronarrative. wordpress.com/2010/01/10/does-making-a-public-commitment-really-help- people-lose-weight/?utm_source=feedburner&utm_medium=feed&utm_ campaign=Feed:+NEURONARRATIVE+(Neuronarrative)&utm_content= Google+Reader)

Dörnyei, Z. (2008). New ways of motivating foreign language learners: Generating vision. *Links, 38*(Winter), 3–4.

Doyle, A. C. (2010). *The sign of the four.* London, England: Bibliolis Books.

Drucker, P. (1954). *The practice of management.* New York, NY: HarperBusiness.

Dweck, C. (2006). *Mindset: The new psychology of success.* New York, NY: Random House.

Dweck, C. S. (2008, Winter). Brainology: Transforming students' motivation to learn. *School Matters.* Retrieved from http://www.nais.org/publications/ ismagazinearticle.cfm?ItemNumber=150509

Dweck, C. (2010). Even geniuses work hard. *Educational Leadership, 68*(1), 16–20. Retrieved from http://www.ascd.org/publications/educational-leadership/ sept10/vol68/num01/Even-Geniuses-Work-Hard.aspx

Easy to visualize goal is powerful motivator to finish a race or a task. (2011, August 15). *ScienceDaily.* Retrieved from http://www.sciencedaily.com/ releases/2011/08/110815143935.htm

Economic & Social Research Council. (2012, January 4). If you plan, then you'll do … but it helps to have a friend. *ScienceDaily*. Retrieved from http://www. sciencedaily.com/releases/2012/01/120104111906.htm

Education professor writes prescription for teachers to succeed: Motivate, motivate, motivate. (2010, September 17). *NIU Today*. Retrieved from http://www.niutoday.info/2010/09/27/education-professor-writes-prescription-for-teachers-to-succeed-motivate-motivate-motivate/

English Language Arts Standards–Anchor Standards. (n.d.). *Common Core: State Standards Initiative*. Retrieved from http://www.corestandards.org/ELA-Literacy

Engraffia, M., Graff, N., Jesuit, S., & Schall, L. (1999). *Improving listening skills through the use of active listening strategies*. (Unpublished master's thesis Saint Xavier University, Chicago, IL. (ERIC Document Reproduction Service No. ED 433573). Retrieved from http://www.eric.ed.gov/PDFS/ED433573.pdf

Ericsson, K. A., Krampe, R. T., & Tesch-Römer, C. (1993). The role of deliberate practice in the acquisition of expert performance. *Psychological Review, 100*(3), 363–406.

Exposure to letters A and F can affect test relationship. (2010, March 9). *ScienceDaily*. Retrieved from http://www.sciencedaily.com/releases/2010/03/100308203306.htm

Ferlazzo, L. (2011). *Helping students motivate themselves: Practical answers to classroom challenges*. Larchmont, NY: Eye On Education.

Ferlazzo, L. (2011, January 28). The best resources showing why we need to be "data-informed" & not "data-driven." [Blog post]. Retrieved from http://larryferlazzo.edublogs.org/2011/01/28/the-best-resources-showing-why-we-need-to-be-data-informed-not-data-driven

Ferlazzo, L. (2011, February 26). The best resources documenting the effectiveness of free voluntary reading. [Blog post]. Retrieved from http://larryferlazzo.edublogs.org/2011/02/26/the-best-resources-documenting-the-effectiveness-of-free-voluntary-reading

Ferlazzo, L. (2012, January 9). Three ways to help students develop intrinsic motivation. *The New York Times*. Retrieved from http://learning.blogs.nytimes.com/2012/01/09/guest-post-helping-students-motivate-themselves/

Ferlazzo, L. (2012, May 19). The best resources for teaching "what if?" history lessons. [Blog post]. Retrieved from http://larryferlazzo.edublogs.org/2012/05/19/the-best-resources-for-teaching-what-if-history-lessons

Ferlazzo, L. (2012, June 4). Response: Several ways we can help students develop good habits. [Blog post]. Retrieved from http://blogs.edweek.org/teachers/classroom_qa_with_larry_ferlazzo/2012/06/response_several_ways_we_can_help_students_develop_good_habits.html

Ferlazzo, L. (2012, July 8). Prof. James Heckman says adolescence is key time to teach (& learn about) self control & perseverance. [Blog post]. Retrieved from http://larryferlazzo.edublogs.org/2012/07/08/prof-james-heckman-says-adolescence-is-key-time-to-teach-learn-about-self-control-perseverance

Ferlazzo, L., & Hull Sypnieski, K. (2012). *The ESL/ELL teacher's survival guide: Ready-to-use strategies, tools, and activities for teaching all levels*. San Francisco, CA: Jossey-Bass.

Fischer, P., Sauer, A., Vogrincic, C., & Weisweiler, S. (2010, December 1). The ancestor effect: Thinking about our genetic origin enhances intellectual performance. *European Journal of Social Psychology, 41*(1), 11–16. Retrieved from http://onlinelibrary.wiley.com/doi/10.1002/ejsp.778/abstract

Flin, R. (2010, May 10). Rudeness at work. *BMJ*. Retrieved from http://www.bmj.com/content/340/bmj.c2480.full?maxtoshow=&hits=10&RESULTFORMAT=&fulltext=Rhona+Flin&searchid=1&FIRSTINDEX=0&sortspec=date&resourcetype=HWCIT

Freeland, C. (2012, April 20). The triumph of the social animal. *Reuters*. Retrieved from http://www.reuters.com/article/2012/04/20/column-freeland-socialanimal-idUSL2E8FKCG320120420

Gallagher, K. (2006). *Teaching adolescent writers*. Portland, ME: Stenhouse Publishers.

Garan, E. M., & DeVoogd, G. (2008). The benefits of Sustained Silent Reading: Scientific research and common sense coverage. *The Reading Teacher, 62*(4), 336–344. Retrieved from http://www.soquelhs.net/library/net%20links/The%20Benefits%20of%20Sustained%20Silent.pdf

Gawande, A. (2012, June 4). Failure and rescue. *The New Yorker*. Retrieved from http://www.newyorker.com/online/blogs/newsdesk/2012/06/atul-gawande-failure-and-rescue.html

Gladwell, M. (2005). *Blink*. New York, NY: Little, Brown and Company.

Gladwell, M. (2012, July 30). Slackers: Alberto Salazar and the art of exhaustion. *The New Yorker*. Retrieved from http://www.newyorker.com/reporting/2012/07/30/120730fa_fact_gladwell?currentPage=2

Glasser, W. (1988). *Choice theory in the classroom*. New York, NY: Harper Perennial.

Goldman, J. G., & Manis, F. R. (2012, March 28). Relationships among cortical thickness, reading skill, and print exposure in adults. doi: 10.1080/10888438.2011.620673. Retrieved from http://www.tandfonline.com/doi/abs/10.1080/10888438.2011.620673?journalCode

Gorman, J. (2012, May 24). "What is" meets "what if": The role of speculation in science. *The New York Times*. Retrieved from http://www.nytimes.com/2012/05/29/science/dogs-and-humans-speculation-and-science.html?_r=4&ref=science

Gosling, S. D., John, O. P., Craik, K. H., & Robins, R. W. (1998). Do people know how they behave? Self-reported act frequencies compared with on-line codings by observers. *Journal of Personality and Social Psychology, 74*(5), 1337–1349.

Got up on the wrong side of the bed? Your work will show it. (2011, April 4). *ScienceDaily*. Retrieved from http://www.sciencedaily.com/releases/2011/04/110404151353.htm

Gots, J. (2011, September 18). Teach with, not "to" the test. *Big Think*. Retrieved from http://bigthink.com/think-tank/teach-with-not-to-the-test?utm_source=Daily+Ideafeed+Newsletter&utm_campaign=bc16aaf0af-Daily_Ideafeed_September_18_2011&utm_medium=email

Grin and bear it! Smiling facilitates stress recovery. (2012, July 30). *Association for Psychological Science*. Retrieved from http://www.psychologicalscience.org/index.php/news/releases/smiling-facilitates-stress-recovery.html

Guthrie, J. T. (2002). Preparing students for high-stakes test taking in reading. In A. E. Farstrup & S. J. Samuels (Eds.), *What research has to say about reading instruction* (3rd ed.). Newark, DE: International Reading Association.

Guttenplan, D. D. (2011, November 20). Motivating students with cash-for-grades incentive. *The New York Times*. Retrieved from http://www.nytimes.com/2011/11/21/world/middleeast/21iht-educLede21.html?pagewanted=all

Halsall, P. (1997). *Modern history sourcebook: Nelson Mandela: Speech on release from prison, 1990*. Retrieved from http://www.fordham.edu/halsall/mod/1990Mandela.html

Halvorson, H. G. (2011, October 31). The art (and science) of giving kids feedback: 3 rules to remember. *Mindset Works*. Retrieved from http://grow.mindsetworks.com/cms/the-art-and-science-of-giving-kids-feedback

Hamzelou, J. (2010, April 23). Placebos work even when you know they're fakes. *NewScientist*. Retrieved from http://www.newscientist.com/article/dn19904-placebos-can-work-even-when-you-know-theyre-fakes.html

Hanford, E. (2011). Don't lecture me: Rethinking how college students learn. *Mind/Shift*. Retrieved from http://blogs.kqed.org/mindshift/2012/02/dont-lecture-me-rethinking-how-college-students-learn-2/

The harm caused by witnessing rudeness. (2009, May 5). *Research Digest*. Retrieved from http://bps-research-digest.blogspot.com/2009/05/harm-caused-by-witnessing-rudeness.html

Hattie, J. (2012). *Visible learning for teachers*. London, England: Routledge.

Heflebower, T. (2009). *Suggested action research protocol*. Marzano Research Laboratory. Retrieved from http://www.marzanoresearch.com/documents/ActionResearchProtocol.pdf

Herbert, W. (2009, February 19). A recipe for motivation: Easy to read, easy to do. *Scientific American*. Retrieved from http://www.scientificamerican.com/article.cfm?id=a-recipe-for-motivation

Hoffman, W., & Friese, M. (2011, April 28). Control yourself! How to keep cravings in check. *Scientific American*. Retrieved from http://www.scientificamerican.com/article.cfm?id=control-yourself&page=3

Holladay, A. (2004, December 10). How old is man? Depends on how you're counting. *USA Today*. Retrieved from http://www.usatoday.com/tech/columnist/aprilholladay/2004-12-10-wonderquest_x.htm

Holt McDougal Literature for Texas, grade 9–12. (n.d.). *HMHEducation.com*. Retrieved from http://hmheducation.com/tx/lit912/authors_1.php

Hout, M., & Elliott, S. W. (Eds.). (2011). *Incentives and test-based accountability in education*. Washington, DC: The National Academies Press. Retrieved from http://www.nap.edu/catalog.php?record_id=12521

How to encourage people to change their own minds. (2012, May 9). *PsyBlog*. Retrieved from http://www.spring.org.uk/2012/05/how-to-encourage-people-to-change-their-own-minds.php?utm_source=feedburner&utm_medium=feed&utm_campaign=Feed%3A+PsychologyBlog+%28PsyBlog%29&utm_content=Google+Reader

How we feel affects what we see. (2009, June 8). *Neurophilosophy*. Retrieved from http://scienceblogs.com/neurophilosophy/2009/06/how_we_feel_affects_what_we_see.php

Hulleman, C. S., & Harackiewicz, J. M. (2009). Promoting interest and performance in high school science classes. *Science, 326*(5958), 1410–1411. Retrieved from http://www.sciencemag.org/content/326/5958/1410.full.pdf

Is bribing students an effective way to boost success? (2012, June 22). Retrieved from http://www.foxbusiness.com/on-air/money-with-melissa-francis/index.html#/v/1702722427001/is-bribing-students-an-effective-way-to-boost-success/?playlist_id=1671716501001

Iyengar, S. (2011, March 11). The "Michigan fish test" and the Middle East. *CNN Opinion*. Retrieved from http://www.cnn.com/2011/OPINION/03/06/iyengar.fish.freedom/index.html?hpt=C1

Jacobson, E. (2008, August 19). When the rude have a 'tude. *USC News*. Retrieved from http://uscnews.usc.edu/business/when_the_rude_have_a_tude.html

Jalongo, M. R. (1995). *Promoting active listening in the classroom*. Retrieved from http://www.questia.com/googleScholar.qst;jsessionid=M2LLqF12cxXChJzL2pjlLQ6SYfTjnS3nszjr2T2KD4nCWTdf86qQ!427202863!1380883283?docId=5002244991

Jarrett, C. (2009, May 5). The harm caused by witnessing rudeness. *Research Digest*. Retrieved from http://bps-research-digest.blogspot.com/2009/05/harm-caused-by-witnessing-rudeness.html

Jensen, E. (2010). Help your students score higher on your upcoming BIG tests. *Brain Based Jensen Learning*. Retrieved from http://www.jensenlearning.com/news/help-your-students-score-higher-on-your-upcoming-big-tests/brain-based-teaching

Jensen, E. (2012, April 3). What research can help your students score higher on the upcoming BIG tests? *Brain Based Jensen Learning*. Retrieved from http://www.jensenlearning.com/news/help-students-score-higher/brain-based-learning

Kahneman, D. (2010, February). Daniel Kahneman: The riddle of experience vs memory. *TED*. Retrieved from http://www.ted.com/talks/lang/eng/daniel_kahneman_the_riddle_of_experience_vs_memory.html

Kang, M. J., Hsu, M., Krajbich, I. M., Loewenstein, G., McClure, S. M., Wang, J. T., & Camerer, C. F. (n.d.). *The hunger for knowledge: Neural correlates of curiosity*. Retrieved from http://lawweb.usc.edu/centers/scip/assets/docs/neuro/Camerer.pdf

Keen, C. (2009, July 29). Rude work behavior hurts job performance of observers as well as victims. *University of Florida News*. Retrieved from http://news.ufl.edu/2009/07/29/rudeness/

Keller, S. (2012a, June 14). How to get senior leaders to change. *Harvard Business Review*. Retrieved from http://blogs.hbr.org/cs/2012/06/how_to_get_senior_leaders_to_c.html?referral=00563&cm_mmc=email-_-newsletter-_-daily_alert-_-alert_date&utm_source=newsletter_daily_alert&utm_medium=email&utm_campaign=alert_date

Keller, S. (2012b, April 26). Increase your team's motivation five-fold. *Harvard Business Review*. Retrieved from http://blogs.hbr.org/cs/2012/04/increase_your_teams_motivation.html

Kepner, T. (2008, March 11). From start, Rodriguez worked to be the best. *The New York Times*. Retrieved from http://www.nytimes.com/2008/03/11/sports/baseball/11yankees.html?_r=1&ref=sports

Kirby, J. (2010, July 7). Rudeness at work can lead to mistakes. *The Independent*. Retrieved from http://www.independent.co.uk/news/uk/home-news/rudeness-at-work-can-lead-to-mistakes-2020369.html

Konnikova, M. (2012a, February 18). Hamlet and the power of beliefs to shape reality. *Scientific American*. Retrieved from http://blogs.scientificamerican.com/literally-psyched/2012/02/18/hamlet-and-the-power-of-beliefs-to-shape-reality/

Konnikova, M. (2012b, April 7). Hunters of myths: Why our brains love origins. *Scientific American*. Retrieved from http://blogs.scientificamerican.com/literally-psyched/2012/04/07/hunters-of-myths-why-our-brains-love-origins/

Konnikova, M. (2012c, April 30). On writing, memory, and forgetting: Socrates and Hemingway take on Zeigarnik. *Scientific American*. Retrieved from http://blogs.scientificamerican.com/literally-psyched/2012/04/30/on-writing-memory-and-forgetting-socrates-and-hemingway-take-on-zeigarnik/

Kosslyn, S. M., & Moulton, S. T. (2008). Mental imagery and implicit memory. In K. D. Markman, W. M. P. Klein, & J. A. Suhr (Eds.), *Handbook of imagination and mental stimulation* (pp. 35–51). London, England: Psychology Press.

Kotz, D. (2012, June 7). How to rewire your brain to be more optimistic. *Daily Dose*. Retrieved from http://www.boston.com/dailydose/2012/06/07/how-rewire-your-brain-more-optimistic/Mk2TNfGfIBknjd4J8XUR3J/story.html

Kristof, K. M. (2009, December 13). Break bad shopping habits to avoid debt hangover. *Los Angeles Times*. Retrieved from http://articles.latimes.com/2009/dec/13/business/la-fi-perfin13-2009dec13

Latham, G. P., & Locke, E. A. (2006). Enhancing the benefits and overcoming the pitfalls of goal setting. *Organizational Dynamics*, *35*(4), 332–340.

Lehrer, J. (2011, October 4). Why do some people learn faster? *Wired*. Retrieved from http://www.wired.com/wiredscience/2011/10/why-do-some-people-learn-faster-2/

Lehrer, J. (2012a, June 8). It's good to be the top banana. *The Wall Street Journal*. Retrieved from http://online.wsj.com/article/SB10001424052702303830204577446831263993506.html?mod=WSJ_LifeStyle_Lifestyle_11_1

Lehrer, J. (2012b, January 9). The willpower trick. *Wired*. Retrieved from http://www.wired.com/wiredscience/2012/01/the-willpower-trick

Lehrer, N. (2010, January 27). Self-control and peer groups. *The Science Blogs*. Retrieved from http://scienceblogs.com/cortex/2010/01/self-control_and_peer_groups.php?utm_source=feedburner&utm_medium=feed&utm_campaign=Feed:+ScienceblogsChannelBrain+(ScienceBlogs+Channel+:+Brain+%26+Behavior)&utm_content=Google+Reader)

L'Engle, M. (1980). *Walking on water: Reflections on faith & art*. Colorado Springs, CO: Harold Shaw Publishers.

Levitt, S. D., List, J. A., Neckermann, S., & Sadoff, S. (2011, September). *The impact of short-term incentives on student performance*. Retrieved from http://bfi.uchicago.edu/events/20111028_experiments/papers/Levitt_List_Neckermann_Sadoff_Short-Term_Incentives_September2011.pdf

Lewis, R., Romi, S., Qui, X., & Katz, Y. J. (2005). Teachers' classroom discipline and student misbehavior in Australia, China and Israel. *Teaching and Teacher Education, 21*(6), 729–741. Retrieved from http://www.sciencedirect.com/science/article/pii/S0742051X05000673

Lopez-Duran, N. (2009, May 28). An apology is more than a word: Effects of apologies on children's emotions. *Child Psychology Research Blog*. Retrieved from http://www.child-psych.org/2009/05/effects-of-apologies-on-childrens-emotions.html

Luscombe, B. (2012, May 8). Why we talk about ourselves: The brain likes it. *Time*. Retrieved from http://healthland.time.com/2012/05/08/why-we-overshare-the-brain-likes-it/

MacInnis, D. (2011, July 10). Human behavior: To resist temptation, forget guilt or shame and think positive. *Los Angeles Times*. Retrieved from http://articles.latimes.com/2011/jul/10/opinion/la-oe-macinnis-selfcontrol-20110710

Mahajan, S. (2011, May 4). Deliberate practice: How education fails to produce expertise. *Freakonomics*. Retrieved from http://www.freakonomics.com/2011/05/04/deliberate-practice-how-education-fails-to-produce-expertise/

Marklein, M. B. (2008, January 23). Employers want new way to judge graduates beyond tests, grades. *USA Today*. Retrieved from http://www.usatoday.com/news/education/2008-01-22-graduate-assessment_N.htm

Markman, A. (2011, March 30). Your beliefs about intelligence affect your beliefs about learning. *Psychology Today*. Retrieved from http://www.psychologytoday.com/blog/ulterior-motives/201103/your-beliefs-about-intelligence-affect-your-beliefs-about-learning

Markman, A. (2012a, May 4). Changing your own mind: What is the best way to convince yourself? *Psychology Today*. Retrieved from http://www.psychologytoday.com/blog/ulterior-motives/201205/changing-your-own-mind

Markman, A. (2012b, May 25). The downside of planning. *Psychology Today*. Retrieved from http://www.psychologytoday.com/blog/ulterior-motives/201205/the-downside-planning

Markman, A. (2012c, January 2). What is the best way to give advice? Retrieved from http://www.smartthinkingbook.com/2012/01/what-is-best-way-to-give-advice.html

Marshall, M. (2011, January 5). Telling vs. asking. *Discipline & parenting without stress*. Retrieved from http://www.marvinmarshall.net/telling-vs-asking

Marzano, R. J. (2007). *The art and science of teaching*. Alexandria, VA: ASCD.

Marzano, R. J. (2011). The perils and promises of discovery learning. *Educational Leadership, 69*(1), 86–87. Retrieved from http://www.ascd.org/publications/educational-leadership/sept11/vol69/num01/The-Perils-and-Promises-of-Discovery-Learning.aspx

Mayo Clinic Staff (2011, May 28). Positive thinking: Reduce stress by eliminating negative self-talk. *Mayo Clinic*. Retrieved from http://www.mayoclinic.com/health/positive-thinking/SR00009

McInnes, A. (2011, June 13). Give your colleagues three compliments for every criticism. Retrieved from http://blogs.forrester.com/andrew_mcinnes/11-06-13-give_your_colleagues_three_compliments_for_every_criticism

McLeod, S. (2012, February 18). Do students need to learn lower-level factual and procedural knowledge before they can do higher-order thinking? *Dangerously Irrelevant*. Retrieved from http://dangerouslyirrelevant.org/2012/02/do-students-need-to-learn-lower-level-factual-and-procedural-knowledge-before-they-can-do-higher-order-thinking.html

Mettetal, G. (2002–2003). Improving teaching through classroom action research. *Essays on Teaching Excellence: Toward the Best in the Academy, 14*(7). Retrieved from http://academic.udayton.edu/FacDev/Newsletters/EssaysforTeachingExcellence/PODvol14/tevol14n7.html

Meyer, D. (2012, July 8). If math is basketball, let students play the game. *Dy/dan*. Retrieved from http://blog.mrmeyer.com/?p=14425

Millman, J. & Pauk, W. (1969). *How to take tests.* New York, NY: McGraw Hill.

Mindlin, A. (2008, March 17). Dos and don'ts of gentle prodding. *The New York Times*. Retrieved from http://www.nytimes.com/2008/03/17/business/17drill.html?_r=1&en=96da4&ex=1363406400&adxnnl=1&oref=slogin&adxnnlx=1304051086-c98AUtWIzR8uaN7NEQZ3tA

Moffitt, T. E., Arseneault, L., Belsky, D., Dickson, N., Hancox, R. J., Harrington, H., Houts, R., et al. (2011, January 24). A gradient of childhood self-control predicts health, wealth, and public safety. *PNAS: Proceedings of the National Academy of Sciences in the United States of America*. doi: 10-1073/pnas.1010076108. Retrieved from http://www.pnas.org/content/early/2011/01/20/1010076108.abstract

Motivator: Create your own motivational posters! (n.d.). *Big Huge Labs*. Retrieved from http://bighugelabs.com/motivator.php

Murayama, K., Pekrun, R., Lichtenfeld, S. and vom Hofe, R. (2012), Predicting Long-Term Growth in Students' Mathematics Achievement: The Unique Contributions of Motivation and Cognitive Strategies. *Child Development*. doi: 10.1111/cdev.12036

Nauert, R. (2010, February 4). Observe a good deed, perform a good deed. *Psych Central*. Retrieved from http://psychcentral.com/news/2010/02/04/observe-a-good-deed-perform-a-good-deed/11180.html

Nelson, D. W., and Knight, A. E. (2010). The power of positive recollections: Reducing test anxiety and enhancing college student efficacy and performance. *Journal of Applied Social Psychology, 40*, 732–745. doi: 10.1111/j.1559-1816.2010.00595.x

O'Brien, M., & Baime, J. (2011, June 20). Teens and stress. *National Science Foundation*. Retrieved from http://www.nsf.gov/news/special_reports/science_nation/teensstress.jsp

OECD. (2010). *PISA 2009 results: Learning to learn—Student engagement, strategies and practices (Volume III)*. http://dx.doi.org/10.1787.9789264083943-en

Omega-3 fatty acids. (n.d.). *The World's Healthiest Foods.* Retrieved from http://www. whfoods.com/genpage.php?tname=nutrient&dbid=84

Oregon State University (2012, August 6). Preschool children who can pay attention more likely to finish college: Early reading and math not predictive of college completion. *ScienceDaily.* Retrieved from http://www.sciencedaily.com / releases/2012/08/120806151405.htm?utm_source=feedburner&utm_medium =feed&utm_campaign=Feed%3A+sciencedaily%2Fmind_brain+%28Science Daily%3A+Mind+%26+Brain+News%29&utm_content=Google+Reader

Organisation for Economic Co-operation and Development. (2010). *PISA 2009 results: Learning to learn – student engagement, strategies, and practices* (Vol. 3). Retrieved from http://books.google.com/books?id=rbzZ7scR130C&pg=PT15&lpg= PT15&dq=perform+at+least+73+points+higher+in+the+pisa+assessmen- t&source=bl&ots=Q5jPd8lBzg&sig=jMvj2BYiunv3Q3EmzjswtkWv JZ0&hl=en&sa=X&ei=0WIcUOKZAYGFiAKEq4H4Dg&ved=0CFwQ6A EwAQ#v=onepage&q=perform%20at%20least%2073%20points%20higher %20in%20the%20pisa%20assessment&f=true

Pappas, P. (2010, January 4). A taxonomy of reflection: Critical thinking for students, teachers, and principals (Part I). Retrieved from http://peterpappas.blogs. com/copy_paste/2010/01/taxonomy-reflection-critical-thinking-students- teachers-principals-.html

Pappas, S. (2012, May 25). Why you should smile at strangers. *The Body Odd.* Retrieved from http://bodyodd.nbcnews.com/_news/2012/05/25/11885101-why- you-should-smile-at-strangers?lite

Park, A. (2012, January 9). Study: Stress shrinks the brain and lowers our abil- ity to cope with adversity. *Time.* Retrieved from http://healthland.time. com/2012/01/09/study-stress-shrinks-the-brain-and-lowers-our-ability-to- cope-with-adversity/#ixzz21gNQOfNp

Pearson, C. (2010, May 15). Sending a message that you don't care. *The New York Times.* Retrieved from http://www.nytimes.com/2010/05/16/jobs/16pre.html?_r=1

Pellegrino, J. W., & Hilton, M. L. (Eds.). (in press). *Education for life and work: Developing transferable knowledge and skills in the 21st Century.* Washington, DC: National Academies Press.

Percentage of employers who want colleges to "place more emphasis" on essential learn- ing outcomes. (n.d.). Retrieved from http://www.aacu.org/leap/documents/ MoreEmphasis_2010.pdf

Perkins, D. (2003, December). Making thinking visible. *New Horizons for Learning.* Retrieved from http://www.newhorizons.org/strategies/thinking/perkins.htm

Persuasive techniques in advertising. (n.d.). *ReadWriteThink.* Retrieved from http:// www.readwritethink.org/classroom-resources/lesson-plans/persuasive- techniques-advertising-1166.html?tab=1#tabs

Pink, D. H. (2009). Dan Pink: The puzzle of motivation. *TED.* Retrieved from http://www.ted.com/talks/dan_pink_on_motivation.html

Pink, D. H. (2011a). *Drive: The surprising truth about what motivates us.* New York, NY: Riverhead Trade.

Pink, D. H. (2011b, August 9). Why progress matters: 6 questions for Harvard's Teresa Amabile. Retrieved from http://www.danpink.com/archives/2011/08/why-progress-matters-6-questions-for-harvards-teresa-amabile?utm_source=twitterfeed&utm_medium=twitter

Pink, D. H. (2012, January 19). Does being reminded of money make you an uncooperative jerk or an independent thinker? Retrieved from http://www.danpink.com/archives/2012/01/does-being-reminded-of-money-make-you-an-uncooperative-jerk-or-an-independent-thinker

Plous, S. (2013). Tips on taking multiple-choice tests. Social Psychology Network. Retrieved from http://www.socialpsychology.org/testtips.htm

Popham, W. J. (n.d.). Standardized testing fails the exam. *Edutopia*. Retrieved from http://www.edutopia.org/f-for-assessment

Positive thinking: Reduce stress by eliminating negative self-talk. (n.d.). *Mayo Clinic*. Retrieved from http://www.mayoclinic.com/health/positive-thinking/SR00009

Priming the customer. (2006, April 6). *Neuromarketing*. Retrieved from http://www.neurosciencemarketing.com/blog/articles/priming-the-customer.htm

Pynchon, T. (1973). *Gravity's Rainbow*. New York, NY: Penguin Press. (http://books.google.com/books?id=GGPm4I3BbxAC&pg=PT281&lpg=PT281&dq=%E2%80%9CIf+they+can+get+you+asking+the+wrong+questions,+they+don't+have+to+worry+about+answers.%E2%80%9D&source=bl&ots=APrJuPNBZD&sig=KJaoXiU9JbZFtv2qKmiDTa9kKFM&hl=en&sa=X&ei=EWsdUJKmKK7piwL-g4C4AQ&ved=0CDAQ6AEwAA#v=onepage&q=%E2%80%9CIf%20they%20can%20get%20you%20asking%20the%20wrong%20questions%2C%20they%20don't%20have%20to%20worry%20about%20answers.%E2%80%9D&f=false

Rathvon, N. (2008). *Effective school interventions: Evidence-based strategies for improving student outcomes*. New York, NY: Guilford Press.

Ravitch, D. (2010, March 15). Pass or fail: The country's love affairs with standardized testing and charter schools is ruining American education. *The New Republic*. Retrieved from http://www.tnr.com/article/politics/pass-or-fail

Reading at 16 linked to better job prospects. (2011, April 8). *University of Oxford*. Retrieved from http://www.ox.ac.uk/media/news_stories/2011/110804.html

Research-based test preparation instruction: Better test scores. (n.d.). *Perfection Learning*. Retrieved from http://www.perfectionlearning.com/images/products/pdfs/bts/bts.researchpaper.pdf

Rest is not idleness. (2012, July 2). *Association for Psychological Science*. Retrieved from http://www.psychologicalscience.org/index.php/news/releases/rest-is-not-idleness-reflection-is-critical-for-development-and-well-being.html

Riddle, T. (2011, March 15). Houseplants make you smarter. *Scientific American*. Retrieved from http://www.scientificamerican.com/article.cfm?id=houseplants-make-you-smarter

Rigoglioso, M. (2008, December). The thought of acquiring power motivates people to act. *Stanford GSB News*. Retrieved from http://www.gsb.stanford.edu/

news/research/fastpower_gruenfeld.html?q=stories/the-thought-acquiring-power-motivates-people-act

Rock, D. (2011, November 10). Praise leads to cheating? *Harvard Business Review*. Retrieved from http://blogs.hbr.org/cs/2011/11/praise_leads_to_cheating.html?referral=00563&cm_mmc=email-_-newsletter-_-daily_alert-_-alert_date&utm_source=newsletter_daily_alert&utm_medium=email&utm_campaign=alert_date

Rodriguez, Tori. (2012, Dec. 5) "How to Use Your Ears to Influence People: Scientific American." *Scientific American*. <http://www.scientificamerican.com/article.cfm?id=how-to-use-your-ears-to-influence-people>

Rothman, J. (2012, May 23). How markets crowd out altruism. *Brainiac*. Retrieved from http://www.boston.com/bostonglobe/ideas/brainiac/2012/05/how_markets_cro.html

Rudeness at work. (2010, May 19). *BMJ, 340*. doi: 10.1136/bmj.c2480

Rudeness at work causes mistakes. (2010, July 6). *ScienceDaily*. Retrieved from http://www.sciencedaily.com/releases/2010/07/100706204709.htm

Savara, S. (n.d.). Writing down your goals – The Harvard written goal study. Fact or fiction? *Personal Development Training with Sid Savara*. Retrieved from http://sidsavara.com/personal-productivity/fact-or-fiction-the-truth-about-the-harvard-written-goal-study

Schlessman, E. (2011, Fall). Patterns and punctuation: Learning to question language. *Rethinking Schools, 26*(1). Retrieved from http://www.rethinkingschools.org//cmshandler.asp?archive/26_01/26_01_schlessman.shtml

Schlosberg, S. (1998, August). Let's get visual: With the right techniques, weight-training success is all in your head. *Moneywatch.com*. Retrieved from http://findarticles.com/p/articles/mi_m1608/is_n8_v14/ai_21032039/

Schunk, D. H. (2003). Self-efficacy for reading and writing: Influence of modeling, goal setting, and self-evaluation. *Reading and Writing Quarterly, 19*, 159–172. Retrieved from http://libres.uncg.edu/ir/uncg/f/D_Schunk_Self_2003.pdf

Schunk, D. H., & Meece, J. L. (2005). Self-efficacy development in adolescences. In F. Pajares & T. Urdan (Eds.), *Self-efficacy beliefs of adolescents* (71–96). Charlotte, NC: Information Age Publishing.

Schwartz, T. (2010, August 24). Six keys to being excellent at anything. Harvard Business *Review*. Retrieved from http://blogs.hbr.org/schwartz/2010/08/six-keys-to-being-excellent-at.html

Self-control instantly replenished by self-affirmation. (2010, March 25). *Psyblog*. Retrieved from http://www.spring.org.uk/2010/03/self-control-instantly-replenished-by-self-affirmation.php?utm_source=feedburner&utm_medium=feed&utm_campaign=Feed:+PsychologyBlog+(PsyBlog)&utm_content=Google+Reader

Sesame Street tells you how to get smarter financially. (2011, June 3). *PBS Newshour*. Retrieved from http://www.pbs.org/newshour/bb/business/jan-june11/makingsense_06-03.html

Seven ways to be good: 6) Form if-then plans. (n.d.). *Research Digest*. Retrieved from http://bps-research-digest.blogspot.com/2011/02/seven-ways-to-be-good-6-form-if-then.html

Shea, C. (2010, November 20). Psychology: Water-cooler power. *The Wall Street Journal*. Retrieved from http://online.wsj.com/article/SB10001424052748704312504575618880445932898.html?mod=WSJ_LifeStyle_Lifestyle_11_50

Shea, C. (2012, January 26). Improving calorie counts. *The Wall Street Journal*. Retrieved from http://blogs.wsj.com/ideas-market/2012/01/26/improving-calorie-counts/?mod=WSJBlog/

Shore, R. (2010, January 29). Visualizing wins could help achieve Olympic gold: Study. *Canada.com*. Retrieved from http://www.canada.com/sports/Visualizing+wins+could+help+achieve+Olympic+gold+Study/2501499/story.html

Shteynberg, G., & Galinsky, A. D. (in press). Implicit coordination: Sharing goals with similar others intensifies goal pursuit. *Journal of Experimental Social Psychology*. Retrieved from https://docs.google.com/a/stanford.edu/viewer?url=http://f.cl.ly/items/0K0I1P0B2m2h2c3r0f3F/Shteynberg:Galinsky%25202011.pdf

Sims, P. (2011, April 5). The Montessori mafia. *The Wall Street Journal*. Retrieved from http://blogs.wsj.com/ideas-market/2011/04/05/the-montessori-mafia

Slattery, J. M. (1998). What do employers look for? Retrieved from http://psy1.clarion.edu/jms/qualifications.html

Slavin, R. E. (2010). Co-operative learning: What makes group-work work? In H. Dumont, D. Istance, & F. Benavides (Eds.), *The nature of learning: Using research to inspire practice* (pp. 161–178). Organisation for Economic Co-operation and Development, Centre for Educational Research and Innovation.

Society for Personality and Social Psychology (2012, January 27). Willpower and desires: Turning up the volume on what you want most. *ScienceDaily*. Retrieved from http://www.sciencedaily.com /releases/2012/01/120130094353.htm

Sousa, D. A. (2005). *How the brain learns* (3rd ed.). Thousand Oaks, CA: Corwin Press.

Sparks, S. D. (2010, December 21). Giving students a say may spur engagement and achievement. *Education Week*. Retrieved from http://blogs.edweek.org/edweek/inside-school-research/2010/12/class_choice_may_spur_student.html?utm_source=twitterfeed&utm_medium=twitter

Sparks, S. D. (2011a, May 26). Panel finds few learning gains from testing movement. *Education Week*. Retrieved from http://www.edweek.org/ew/articles/2011/05/26/33academy.h30.html?tkn=WMZFS%2FW96v61G219atrR%2F52%2BF7dt13KpDqLj&cmp=clp-edweek&utm_source=feedburner&utm_medium=feed&utm_campaign=Feed%3A+EducationWeekWidgetFeed+%28Education+Week%3A+Free+Widget+Feed%29&utm_content=Twitter

Sparks, S. D. (2011b, October 19). Study: Adolescents can see dramatic IQ changes. *Education Week*. Retrieved from http://blogs.edweek.org/edweek/inside-school-research/2011/10/intelligence_quotient_or_iq_te.html

Sparks, S. D. (2012, May 15). Studies on multitasking highlight value of self-control. *Education Week*. Retrieved from http://www.edweek.org/ew/

articles/2012/05/16/31multitasking_ep.h31.html?tkn=QZVF6b9MEj75LQ
j0AlTWzcEwLc0ua5WzXiGq&cmp=ENL-EU-NEWS1

Spears, T. (2009, August 20). *One rude worker poisons a whole office, study finds.* Retrieved from http://noworkplacebullies.com/yahoo_site_admin/assets/docs/Onerudeworkerpoisons.234100348.pdf

The Standards: English Language Arts Standards. (2010). *Common Core State Standards Initiative: Preparing America's students for college and career.* Retrieved from http://www.corestandards.org/the-standards/english-language-arts-standards

STAR/CST tips and scoring chart. (n.d.). Retrieved from http://teachers.sduhsd.net/cvadmin/CSTtips.htm

Strauss, V. (2011, July 6). Letting teachers re-invent their own wheel. *The Washington Post.* Retrieved from http://www.washingtonpost.com/blogs/answer-sheet/post/letting-teachers-re-invent-their-own-wheel/2011/07/06/gIQAM9lQ1H_blog.html?wprss=answer-sheet

Stress. (n.d.). *TeensHealth.* Retrieved from http://kidshealth.org/teen/your_mind/emotions/stress.html?tracking=81452_A#

Stress: Constant stress puts your health at risk. (n.d.). *Mayo Clinic.* Retrieved from http://www.mayoclinic.com/health/stress/SR00001

Studies show stress can reshape the brain. (2008, November 19). *The Guardian.* Retrieved from http://www.guardian.co.uk/science/2008/nov/19/brain-stress-research-reshape

Sutton, B. (2008, August). It isn't just a myth: A little thanks goes a long way. *Bob Sutton: Work matters.* Retrieved from http://bobsutton.typepad.com/my_weblog/2010/08/it-isnt-just-a-myth-a-little-thanks-goes-a-long-way.html

Svenson, O. (1981). Are we all less risky and more skillful than our fellow drivers? *Acta Psychologica, 47,* 143–148.

Ten minutes of talking improves memory and test performance. (2007, November 1). *ScienceDaily.* Retrieved by http://www.sciencedaily.com/releases/2007/10/071029172856.htm

Thalheimer, W. (2006, May 1). People remember 10%, 20% … oh really? *Will at Work Learning.* Retrieved from http://www.willatworklearning.com/2006/05/people_remember.html

This is your brain on no self-control. (2012, June 6). *Newswise.* Retrieved from http://www.newswise.com/articles/this-is-your-brain-on-no-self-control

Tugend, A. (2012, March 23). Praise is fleeting, but brickbats we recall. *The New York Times.* Retrieved from http://www.nytimes.com/2012/03/24/your-money/why-people-remember-negative-events-more-than-positive-ones.html?pagewanted=all

University of New Hampshire (2012, February 10). Controlling parents more likely to have delinquent children. *ScienceDaily.* Retrieved from http://www.sciencedaily.com /releases/2012/02/120210105901.htm

Usher, A., & Kober, N. (2012). *Can money or other rewards motivate students?* Washington, DC: Center on Education Policy, George Washington University. Retrieved from http://www.cep-dc.org/displayDocument.cfm?DocumentID=405

Viadero, D. (2010, August 16). Studies show why students study is as important as what. *Education Week*. Retrieved from http://blogs.edweek.org/edweek/inside-school-research/2010/08/studies_show_why_students_stud.html

Wallop, H. (2011, April 8). Reading as teenager gets you a better job. *The Telegraph*. Retrieved from http://www.telegraph.co.uk/foodanddrink/8435031/Reading-as-teenager-gets-you-a-better-job.html

Walter Mischel's marshmallow study. (2011, February 20). *BBC Mind Changers*. Retrieved from http://www.bbc.co.uk/programmes/b00ymjpr

Walton, A. G. (2012, January 13). The connection between good nutrition and good cognition. *The Atlantic*. Retrieved from http://www.theatlantic.com/health/archive/2012/01/the-connection-between-good-nutrition-and-good-cognition/251227/

Want to be happier? Be more grateful. (2008, November 27). *ScienceDaily*. Retrieved from http://www.child-psych.org/2009/05/effects-of-apologies-on-childrens-emotions.html

Washburn, K. (2009, June 9). Learning from mistakes takes the right feedback. *Edurati Review*. Retrieved from http://www.eduratireview.com/2009/06/i-slammed-my-foot-and-to-my-surprise.html

Washburn, K. (2012, January 10). Patterns: Learning, thinking, creating. *Clerestory Learning*. Retrieved from http://blog.clerestorylearning.com/patterns-learning-thinking-creating

Weinstein, N., & Ryan, R. M. (2010). When helping helps: Autonomous motivation for prosocial behavior and its influence on well-being for the helper and recipient. *Journal of Personality and Social Psychology*, *98*, 222–244. Retrieved from http://www.selfdeterminationtheory.org/faculty?id=136

What happens when you evaluate students by gratefulness and materialism? (2010, July 12). Retrieved from http://www.bakadesuyo.com/what-happens-when-you-evaluate-students-by-gr?utm_source=feedburner&utm_medium=feed&utm_campaign=Feed:+bakadesuyo+(Barking+up+the+wrong+tree)

What's an easy way to strengthen your relationships? (2010, August 2). Retrieved from http://www.bakadesuyo.com/whats-an-easy-way-to-strengthen-your-relation?utm_source=feedburner&utm_medium=feed&utm_campaign=Feed:+bakadesuyo+(Barking+up+the+wrong+tree)

Whitson, T. (n.d.). Does chewing gum make students smarter? *Tony's curriculog*. Retrieved from http://www.curriculog.org/2007/04/15/does-chewing-gum-make-students-smarter/index.html

Why is a touch on the arm so persuasive? (2011, July 6). *Research Digest*. Retrieved from http://bps-research-digest.blogspot.co.uk/2011/07/why-is-touch-on-arm-so-persuasive.html

Wiesel, E. (2000). *Night*. New York, NY: Glencoe/McGraw-Hill.

Wikipedia improves students' work: Students become much more concerned with accuracy when their research is posted online, study finds. (2011, May 31). *ScienceDaily*. Retrieved from http://www.sciencedaily.com/releases/2011/05/110531102708.htm

Will we succeed? The science of self-motivation. (2010, May 28). *E! Science News*. Retrieved from http://esciencenews.com/articles/2010/05/28/will.we.succeed.the.science.self.motivation

Willingham, D. (2011, Summer). Can teachers increase students' self-control? *American Educator*. Retrieved from http://www.aft.org/pdfs/americaneducator/summer2011/Willingham.pdf

Willingham, D. (2012, April 24). Does chewing gum help you concentrate? Maybe briefly. Retrieved from http://www.danielwillingham.com/1/post/2012/04/does-chewing-gum-help-you-concentrate-maybe-briefly.html

Wolf, M., & Barzillai, M. (2009). The importance of deep reading. *Educational Leadership, 66*(6), 32–37. Retrieved from http://www.ascd.org/ascd/pdf/journals/ed_lead/el200903_wolf.pdf

Wolfe, P. (2001). *Brain matters: Translating research into classroom practice.* Alexandria, VA: ASCD.

Wormeli, R. (2004). *Summarization in any subject: 50 techniques to improve student learning.* Alexandria, VA: ASCD

Writing about exam worries for 10 minutes improves student results. (n.d.). *Discover Magazine*. Retrieved from http://blogs.discovermagazine.com/notrocketscience/2011/01/13/writing-about-exam-worries-for-10-minutes-improves-student-results/?utm_source=feedburner&utm_medium=feed&utm_campaign=Feed%3A+NotRocketScience+%28Not+Exactly+Rocket+Science%29

Ybarra, O., Bernstein, E., Winkielman, P., Keller, M. C., Manis, M., Chan, E., & Rodriguez, J. (2008). Mental exercising through simple socializing: Social interaction promotes general cognitive functioning. *Personality and Social Psychology Bulletin, 34,* 248–259. Retrieved from http://psy2.ucsd.edu/~pwinkiel/ybarra-burnstein-winkielman_socializing-pspb-2008.pdf

The Young Foundation. (2011). "Creating a more equal and productive Britain" – A lecture by Professor James Heckman. *Vimeo*. Retrieved from http://vimeo.com/24274324

The Zeigarnik Effect. (2011, February 8). *Psyblog*. Retrieved from http://www.spring.org.uk/2011/02/the-zeigarnik-effect.php

Zhao, Y. (2011, March 27). Race to self destruction: A history lesson for education reformers. Retrieved from http://zhaolearning.com/2011/03/27/race-to-self-destruction-a-history-lesson-for-education-reformers/

Zinn, H. (2002). *You can't be neutral on a moving train: A personal history of our times.* Boston, MA: Beacon Press.